AI Implementation for Small Businesses

The Small Business AI Advantage - How to Automate, Scale, and Compete with Fortune 500s Using Free and Low-Cost AI Tools

Nicci Brochard
&
Dr. Ben Chuba

AI Implementation for Small Businesses

The Small Business AI Advantage - How to Automate, Scale, and Compete with Fortune 500s Using Free and Low-Cost AI Tools

CROSSBORDER

New York, London, Quebec

Contents

Introduction 1

Chapter 1: Embracing AI – The New Frontier for Small

Businesses 3

The AI Revolution Reaches Main Street 3
Opportunities and Challenges for SMEs 5
Leveling the Playing Field with AI 9
Democratization of AI Tools (Free and Low-Cost Solutions) 14

Chapter 2: Building Your Small Business AI Advantage

(Automate, Scale, Compete) 20

Identifying High-Impact Automation Opportunities 21
Selecting the Right Low-Cost Tools and Platforms 24
Implementing on a Budget – Pilot Projects and Team Training 29
Measuring Success and Scaling Up 33

Chapter 3: AI in Retail – Modernizing the Small Shop Experience

.... 39

Personalized Customer Engagement and Service 39
AI-Powered Chatbots for 24/7 Service 40
Personalized Product Recommendations 41
Smart Inventory Management and Supply Chain Optimization 42
AI Demand Forecasting 43
Optimizing Stock Levels and Reducing Waste 44
Reliability and Customer Satisfaction 44
Targeted Marketing and Dynamic Pricing Strategies 45
AI-Driven Targeted Marketing 46
Dynamic Pricing for Competitiveness 47
Case Study – Boutique Retailer Thrives with AI: TrendThreads 48

Chapter 4: AI in Consulting and Professional Services –

Amplifying Your Expertise 51

Accelerating Research and Data Analysis...51
Automating Administrative and Routine Tasks...56
Enhancing Client Engagement and Value Delivery.......................................62
Case Study – Transforming a Small Firm through AI....................................68

Chapter 5: AI in Digital Marketing – Doing More With Less 76

Content Creation and Creative Design at Scale..76
Precision Targeting and Analytics (Marketing to the Right Audience)......78
Social Media Automation and Customer Engagement...................................80
Case Study – AI-Powered Marketing Campaign Success.............................84

Chapter 6: AI in Manufacturing and Operations – Smart, Lean, and Agile 88

Automation and Robotics for Small-Scale Production..................................88
Predictive Maintenance and Quality Control...91
Optimizing Production Planning and Supply Chain......................................95
Case Study – Small Manufacturer Goes High-Tech......................................98

Chapter 7: Ethics, Data Privacy, and Regulatory Compliance – Safeguarding Your AI Strategy 104

Ethical AI Use and Bias Mitigation...104
Protecting Customer Data and Privacy...107
Navigating the Regulatory Landscape for AI..113
Building Trust through Transparency and Accountability..........................118

Epilogue...123

Introduction

Small business owners face an unprecedented opportunity. While Fortune 500 companies struggle with bureaucratic AI implementations costing millions, you possess something they desperately lack: agility. The same nimbleness that allows you to pivot quickly, make decisions without committee approvals, and adapt to market changes overnight now becomes your greatest competitive weapon in the AI revolution.

The corporate giants are drowning in their own complexity. Their AI initiatives require months of planning, executive buy-in, and massive infrastructure investments. Meanwhile, you can implement powerful AI solutions this afternoon using nothing more than your laptop and an internet connection. The playing field has never been more level.

This transformation runs deeper than simple automation. AI tools available today—many completely free—can handle tasks that would have required entire departments just five years ago. Customer service chatbots that never sleep. Content creation systems that produce marketing materials in minutes. Data analysis tools that uncover insights your competitors miss. Inventory management systems that predict demand with startling accuracy.

The small business advantage extends beyond speed and cost. You know your customers personally. You understand your market intimately. You can spot opportunities that massive corporations overlook. AI amplifies these natural strengths, turning your deep market knowledge into automated systems that work around the clock.

Throughout these pages, you'll discover exactly which tools to use, how to implement them without technical expertise, and most importantly, how to leverage AI's power while maintaining the personal touch that makes small businesses irreplaceable.

The AI revolution rewards the bold and the quick. Fortune 500 companies will eventually catch up, but by then, you'll already be miles ahead. Your moment is now. Your competitive advantage awaits. Let's begin building your AI-powered future.

Ben and I (Nicci) thank you immensely for choosing our book. We promise you a great time ahead.

Chapter 1

Embracing AI – The New Frontier for Small Businesses

A rtificial intelligence isn't the exclusive playground of tech giants anymore. Walk down any Main Street, and you might be surprised to find AI quietly at work in bakeries, boutiques, and local service firms. Small business owners are discovering that AI isn't some distant, high-tech concept reserved for Silicon Valley – it's a practical tool they can use right now. In this chapter, we explore how AI has reached Main Street, what opportunities it brings (and challenges it poses) for small and mid-sized enterprises (SMEs), and how even the most budget-conscious entrepreneur can leverage free and low-cost AI tools. By the end, you'll see why adopting AI is not just feasible but essential for automating, scaling, and competing in today's market. Let's dive in, with a conversational and motivational look at AI's small business advantage.

The AI Revolution Reaches Main Street

Not long ago, artificial intelligence seemed like a luxury only huge corporations could afford. They had the data, the experts, and the money to experiment with machine learning and advanced algorithms. But times have changed. AI's revolution has officially reached Main Street. Thanks to cloud computing and a wave of user-friendly AI platforms, AI is now accessible and affordable for small businesses, essentially tilting the playing field in favor of small entrepreneurs. What does this mean? It means the corner shop or local startup can now tap into AI capabilities that once required the resources of a Fortune 500 firm. The barriers of cost and complexity have come crashing down, opening the door for small businesses to join the AI movement.

This shift isn't just hype – it's reflected in the attitudes and actions of business owners. A recent survey of nearly 1,000 small businesses found that 82% believe adopting AI is essential to stay competitive in today's environment. In other words, the vast majority of entrepreneurs recognize that AI is key to keeping up with customer expectations and nimble competitors. And many aren't waiting around: about 1 in 4 small businesses have already integrated AI into their daily operations, using it for things like automating emails, engaging customers online, or optimizing inventory. Another study shows a similar trend – 40% of U.S. small businesses are already using generative AI for tasks such as gathering customer insights and managing customer relationships. Clearly, AI is no longer the province of tech giants; it's becoming standard practice on Main Street.

Perhaps most telling is how small business owners themselves talk about this change. They often express amazement at how AI tools have become within reach. As one entrepreneur put it, "AI isn't just for tech giants anymore – it's for everyone". Whether you're running a local bakery or a home-based online shop, these tools can make life simpler and business smoother. The mindset shift is real: instead of viewing AI as something abstract or intimidating, small business owners are beginning to see it as another handy tool – as familiar as an Excel spreadsheet or a smartphone app – that can help them get ahead. The AI revolution has truly arrived on Main Street, and it's leveling the technology playing field between the little guys and the big players.

Of course, this newfound accessibility of AI is a game-changer for how all businesses operate. Even a family-run store can now leverage AI-driven insights or automation that improve efficiency and customer experience. Imagine a mom-and-pop retail shop using an AI-powered chatbot on its website to answer customer questions 24/7, or a two-person marketing agency using machine learning to analyze social media trends overnight. These things are happening today. By embracing AI, small businesses are finding they can serve customers faster, market themselves smarter, and make decisions more data-driven than ever before – all at a fraction of the cost it would have taken a decade ago. Artificial intelligence has reached the mainstream of small business, and it's opening opportunities that were once unimaginable for a company with a modest budget.

Opportunities and Challenges for SMEs

AI offers an enticing wealth of opportunities for small and mid-sized enterprises. Imagine automating those repetitive back-office tasks that eat up hours – invoicing, scheduling, data entry – so you and your team can focus on more strategic work. AI makes this possible. Or consider the heaps of data even a small business accumulates (sales figures, website traffic, customer feedback) – within these numbers are valuable customer trends and insights, if only you had time to uncover them. AI can help with that too, by quickly analyzing data and highlighting patterns a human might miss. In short, small businesses stand to gain efficiency, insight, and productivity from AI. In practice, this can mean faster operations, better decision-making, and even higher profits. In fact, surveys show that over 90% of small business owners agree AI tools save time and boost profitability for their companies. By automating routine processes and providing smarter analytics, AI lets a lean team accomplish far more than they could on their own.

Concretely, AI is already helping SMEs enhance a variety of functions. For example, it can improve customer experience by powering chatbots or personalized recommendations – giving customers quick, tailored service without hiring an army of support reps. AI can assist in forecasting and planning, helping a business owner predict cash flow or inventory needs with greater accuracy. It can even help sniff out anomalies like fraudulent transactions or accounting errors before they become big problems. The payoff can be significant: one study found that businesses using AI saw a *12-point increase* in the likelihood of profit growth compared to non-adopters. The message is clear – those who leverage AI's strengths often find themselves growing faster and operating more efficiently than those who don't.

Yet, alongside these opportunities come unique challenges for small and mid-sized businesses. SMEs don't have the same deep pockets or in-house tech teams that large corporations do, which can make AI adoption tricky. Limited budgets are a reality – unlike a big firm, a small business might not have hundreds of thousands of dollars to spend on custom AI development or pricey software licenses. Hiring AI talent is another hurdle: data scientists and machine learning engineers are in high demand, and many small companies struggle to attract or afford such specialists. In fact, research shows SMEs are much more likely than large companies to report a lack of AI-skilled talent on their teams. Additionally, smaller firms may have smaller data sets to work with. AI systems often learn from lots of data, and a local business simply might not generate the volume of data a Fortune 500 company does. This raises concerns about whether their AI solutions will be as effective or accurate. And let's not forget the learning curve – 47% of small business owners have said not knowing how to use AI tools is a major barrier to adoption. It's not that they're uninterested; rather, they're unsure where to start or how to integrate AI into their existing operations. Other common worries include whether new AI tools will play nicely with the software they already use (over 30% cite compatibility issues) and whether using AI could introduce security or privacy risks (around 26% express this concern).

All these challenges can make the AI journey feel daunting to a time-strapped entrepreneur. However, the good news is that these hurdles can be overcome – and they don't have to hinder innovation. How can small businesses clear the path to AI adoption despite constraints? One key strategy is to start with user-friendly AI services that don't require a PhD in computer science to operate. Today, there are many AI tools designed with non-technical users in mind, sporting intuitive interfaces and simple setup processes. For example, instead of building a machine learning model from scratch, a small business might use a pre-built AI service (like a platform that analyzes customer reviews and automatically highlights the main sentiments). Many of these services are as easy to sign up for as any cloud software – meaning you can experiment with AI without needing an in-house expert. Indeed, a Salesforce survey found 75% of small businesses are already experimenting with AI in some form, often through such accessible platforms, even if they haven't fully rolled it out. The experimentation phase is a great way to get comfortable with AI on a small scale before making bigger commitments.

Another approach to overcoming resource limitations is partnering with outside experts or consultants on a flexible basis. If you can't afford a full-time data scientist, you might hire a freelance AI specialist for a short-term project or consult with an AI-focused agency that understands small business needs. This can be surprisingly cost-effective – rather than bearing the salary of a new department, you pay only for the expertise and time you need. There's a growing ecosystem of AI consultants who specialize in helping SMEs identify affordable AI solutions and implement them effectively. They can guide you in choosing the right tools, integrating AI with your current workflows, and training your team to use it. In essence, they bridge the knowledge gap so that lack of in-house tech skills doesn't mean missing out on AI's benefits. Small businesses can also tap into public and private programs aimed at supporting AI adoption – for instance, some large tech companies offer initiatives to help smaller firms get on board with AI, and local business associations or government agencies sometimes host training workshops or grants. (Microsoft's recent "AI for SMBs" initiative is one example of big tech reaching out to small business users with tailored tools and resources.) Additionally, investing in a bit of employee upskilling can go a long way. Many free or low-cost online courses can teach your staff the basics of AI and data analytics. By empowering your existing team with some AI know-how, you reduce the intimidation factor and build internal capacity to innovate.

In summary, while SMEs face real challenges in adopting AI – be it budget, expertise, or data – these challenges are not insurmountable. Starting small, leaning on user-friendly tools, and seeking help when needed can propel even a tiny company into the AI age. Remember, every big innovation comes with a learning curve. The key is not to be paralyzed by what you *don't* have, but to leverage what you *do* have: creativity, agility, and the growing array of accessible AI resources. With the right approach, constraints can be navigated, and your small business can reap the efficiency and insight that AI promises without breaking the bank or stalling operations. The opportunity is enormous, and those who tackle the challenges head-on will find AI becoming a trusted ally in their business growth.

Leveling the Playing Field with AI

One of AI's greatest promises for entrepreneurs is its potential to level the playing field between small businesses and large corporations. Traditionally, big companies held almost all the advantages – huge marketing budgets, armies of analysts poring over data, and custom IT systems giving them insights and efficiencies unavailable to smaller rivals. But AI is changing that dynamic. When properly harnessed, AI can be "a great equalizer for small businesses", allowing a 10-person company to perform tasks and make data-driven decisions on par with far larger organizations. In fact, some researchers suggest that generative AI could help close the technology and performance gap between small and large firms in the coming years. This is an exciting development: it means that being small is no longer an inherent disadvantage in certain aspects of competition. With AI tools at their disposal, small businesses can be just as quick, clever, and personalized as the big guys – and sometimes even more agile.

How exactly does AI help bridge the gap? Consider the realm of data analytics. A Fortune 500 retailer might employ a full team of data scientists to analyze market trends and customer behaviors, extracting insights to refine their strategy. A few years ago, no corner shop could dream of doing the same – they simply didn't have the resources or technology. But now, even modestly sized businesses can use AI-powered analytics tools to crunch numbers and reveal trends in their sales or customer data. AI systems can analyze vast data sets in minutes, something that would take humans weeks, allowing a small firm to understand its market and customers almost as deeply as a large corporation with a dedicated research division. This is the power of automation and machine learning: it does the heavy lifting of analysis, enabling small companies to base their decisions on evidence and patterns rather than guesswork. The playing field in strategic decision-making starts to even out when both big and small can draw on rich insights.

Another area where AI levels the field is customer outreach and personalization. Large companies like Amazon or Netflix are famous for their personalized recommendations and targeted marketing, driven by sophisticated AI algorithms. It's a competitive edge that historically came from their scale and tech investment. But today, AI-driven marketing and personalization aren't exclusive to giants. For example, a small e-commerce business can implement AI that tracks customer preferences and browsing behavior, then automatically recommends products or sends tailored marketing emails – effectively creating a personalized shopping experience just like the one customers get on major platforms. AI tools make it possible to segment customers and customize communications with an efficiency and precision that a tiny marketing team could never achieve on its own. Suddenly, the local boutique can engage in one-to-one marketing that rivals what the multinational chain down the road is doing, forging strong customer loyalty through relevance and personal touch.

Automation and efficiency gains from AI also help small businesses punch above their weight. Think about customer service: a large company might have a call center operating 24/7. A small business can't afford that – but with AI chatbots and virtual assistants, they *can* offer round-the-clock support without hiring an overnight shift. AI chatbots use natural language processing to handle common inquiries, book appointments, or troubleshoot basic issues, so customers get immediate service at any hour. This means a five-person company's website can provide help to customers overseas late at night, much as a global corporation would – a feat unimaginable before AI. Similarly, automation of internal processes (like order processing or document handling) can dramatically shrink the time needed to do tasks. One real-world example is a small lending company that used AI to process and review loan documents at lightning speed, cutting a task that took days down to mere hours. By doing so, they close the efficiency gap with bigger competitors – deals get done faster, customers are happier, and the small firm can handle a higher volume of business with the same headcount. These types of wins show how being agile and AI-powered can let a smaller player outmaneuver larger ones who might be slower to change.

Let's look at a few real examples of entrepreneurs leveraging AI to compete with industry titans. In one case, a solo real estate professional developed her own AI-driven marketing assistant to automate lead tracking and client follow-ups – something that gave her the capabilities of an entire support team at virtually no extra cost. In another, a small commercial real estate lender named Nectar has built machine learning tools to swiftly analyze financial documents and assess loans. This has allowed them to streamline their operations and close deals faster than traditional lenders, even though they focus on smaller transactions. According to the company's founder, using AI to synthesize large amounts of data quickly lets them operate with an efficiency similar to much larger financial institutions. In fact, Nectar's AI tools reduced one of their key processes (preparing an underwriting memo) from 3–5 days down to a couple of hours. That speed is a competitive advantage directly enabled by AI, empowering a relatively small firm to match or exceed the turnaround times of far bigger banks.

These examples underscore a broader point: AI-powered analytics and automation enable even a 10-person company to act like a 100-person company in certain respects. By adopting AI, small businesses can scale their capabilities without scaling their headcount at the same rate. This doesn't mean a small business will suddenly have the same market muscle as a Fortune 500, but it dramatically narrows the gap in specific functional areas. In effect, AI grants "superpowers" that compensate for a lack of manpower or legacy data. It allows small businesses to be more agile and data-driven, making decisions quickly based on real-time information and automating low-level tasks so they can focus on creative, high-level strategy. Large corporations often struggle with bureaucracy and inertia; meanwhile, a small company that's lean and fueled by AI insights can pivot faster and personalize its offerings more deftly.

The democratization of AI is thus leveling the playing field. When nearly anyone can use advanced tools that once were exclusive to big companies, competition becomes more about who can use insights smarter and move faster, rather than simply who has deeper pockets. As PayPal's small business division General Manager noted, when AI is accessible and built for real-life use, it becomes a great equalizer that allows small businesses to reap benefits in personalization, fulfillment, and customer discovery much like their larger counterparts. The takeaway is empowering: armed with AI, a savvy small business can not only hold its own against bigger competitors but sometimes even outmaneuver them by being more innovative and customer-attuned. In the following chapters, we'll see more real-world cases of entrepreneurs using AI to punch above their weight. But first, let's examine the array of

AI tools that have made this all possible – many of which are either free or very affordable – proving that cost is no longer a barrier to entry in the AI arena.

Democratization of AI Tools (Free and Low-Cost Solutions)

Perhaps the most encouraging development in recent years is the explosion of free and low-cost AI tools available to small businesses. There was a time when implementing AI meant hiring expensive developers to build custom systems or paying for enterprise software licenses that could run into the tens of thousands of dollars. Not anymore. Today, powerful AI solutions are available for as little as the cost of a monthly software subscription, and many come with free versions or trial periods. In short, the tools of AI have been democratized – practically any small business owner with an internet connection can dip their toes into AI without a massive investment. As one tech consultancy put it, *"Artificial intelligence isn't just for big companies with huge budgets anymore. These days, SMBs can also use AI to make their operations smoother, enhance customer experiences, and grow faster – all without spending a fortune."* That's an incredibly empowering statement. It means cost doesn't have to hold you back from innovating. Even on a shoestring budget, you can start leveraging AI in your business.

The marketplace of AI tools for small business is rich and growing by the day. There are free or freemium chatbot frameworks, drag-and-drop machine learning platforms, and affordable cloud AI services that charge only for what you use. Many AI providers offer free tiers or low-cost plans specifically to encourage small companies to experiment and see value early. For example, you can sign up and build a basic chatbot for your website at no charge using certain platforms, only paying if you need advanced features or high volumes of messages. Likewise, major cloud vendors like Amazon, Google, and Microsoft all have pay-as-you-go AI services, meaning you can access their powerful AI infrastructure and models and only pay pennies or dollars for the small amounts you actually use. There's no need to buy servers or advanced hardware; a solo entrepreneur can literally rent an AI's brainpower by the hour. This cloud-based, on-demand model has been a game-changer, because it removed the upfront cost barrier. Want to do image recognition or natural language processing? You can utilize the same kind of AI tech that big companies use, through cloud APIs, and spend perhaps a few dollars a month or take advantage of a free trial.

To make this more concrete, let's highlight some popular budget-friendly AI tools that small businesses are already using to great effect. These tools show that powerful AI solutions are often available for free or at minimal cost:

- OpenAI's ChatGPT: This AI chatbot and writing assistant is a versatile, surprisingly free tool (with an option to pay for faster service) that many small firms use for everything from drafting marketing copy to handling initial customer service queries. ChatGPT's familiar chat-style interface makes it easy to generate content, brainstorm ideas, or get answers to questions without any special technical skill. It can act like your on-demand copywriter or support agent, helping write product descriptions, social media posts, or even answering frequently asked questions for customers – all at essentially zero cost for the basic version.

- Canva (Magic Design): Canva is a graphic design platform popular with small businesses, and its Magic Design feature uses AI to help create visual content. With free and low-cost plans, Canva's AI can suggest design layouts, generate unique graphics, and even tailor marketing materials to your brand style. This means even if you don't have a graphic designer on staff, you can quickly produce professional-looking flyers, social media images, or presentations. It's like having a creative assistant that works with you to make eye-catching visuals, saving you time and money on design work.

- Zapier: Zapier is an automation tool that isn't AI in itself, but it recently introduced AI-powered features and integrations that let you connect different apps and automate workflows with ease. It offers a free plan for basic use. Small businesses leverage Zapier's AI to do things like automatically sort incoming emails, update spreadsheets, or send notifications based on certain triggers – tasks that might otherwise require a human or a lot of coding. With minimal setup, Zapier can function as a "glue" between your everyday apps (like Gmail, QuickBooks, Shopify, etc.), with AI handling the logic in between. It enables even non-technical users to set up powerful automations, streamlining operations without any custom software development.

These are just a few examples; the AI tool landscape includes everything from free analytics tools to AI scheduling assistants, but the ones above illustrate how diverse and accessible the options have become.

Importantly, many of these tools come with free tiers or trial periods, so you can test them out before committing any money. For instance, you might try ChatGPT's free version to see how it can help with writing tasks, or use a limited version of an AI scheduling app to gauge its usefulness. If you find value, upgrading to a paid plan often costs on the order of $10 to $50 per month, which is a trivial expense compared to the value of time saved or new business generated. In essence, powerful AI capabilities have been packaged into affordable, subscription-based software services – putting them within reach of any serious small business owner. It's the same model as subscribing to, say, a $20/month business software, but here that subscription could give you access to AI-driven insights or automation that dramatically boost your productivity. The message is clear: cost is no longer a show-stopper when it comes to implementing AI.

Another aspect of the democratization of AI is the availability of open-source tools and community resources. If you or someone on your team is a bit tech-savvy, you can take advantage of free open-source AI frameworks and models that are shared online. Communities of developers have released AI models for tasks like language translation, image recognition, or predictive analytics that anyone can download and use. This means a determined small business owner could, for example, build a custom chatbot using an open-source library without paying a dime for the software (just the time to set it up). Even if that's too technical for you personally, the existence of these open resources has another benefit: it drives down cost in the industry overall and often leads to low-cost commercial offerings built on those open tools. Plus, you can hire developers on a contract basis to tailor these open-source AI solutions to your needs, often at a far lower cost than starting from scratch.

Perhaps one of the most significant free AI resources is the pool of pre-trained models available through services. Platforms like ChatGPT that we mentioned are a great example – they come *pre-trained on vast amounts of data*, which is why you don't need to supply your own huge dataset or computing power to get useful results. In effect, platforms like ChatGPT eliminate the need for you to have large datasets, powerful computers, or specialized AI talent in-house. They've done the heavy lifting behind the scenes. As a small business, you simply tap into that intelligence through a user-friendly interface or an API. This drastically lowers the technical barriers. You don't need to reinvent the wheel or invest in supercomputers; you just leverage what's already been built and offered, often at minimal cost. The result: a truly democratic AI landscape where a two-person startup has access to AI capabilities nearly as advanced as those a tech behemoth employs – the difference being the startup is renting those capabilities on-demand instead of owning them outright.

In summary, the democratization of AI tools means that any small business owner who is curious and proactive can begin using AI here and now, without budgetary barriers. Free and low-cost solutions abound for various needs – whether you want to automate your marketing, streamline customer service, or get better analytics to drive decisions. The playing field has opened up, and the cost of entry to the AI world has fallen dramatically. It's an invitation for innovators and late adopters alike: you no longer have to ask "Can I afford AI?" but rather "Which AI tools should I try first?" The power to automate, scale, and compete with larger firms is at your fingertips, often for less than the cost of your monthly office coffee budget.

By embracing these accessible AI tools, small businesses can truly gain an advantage. The rest of this book will delve into how you can strategically implement these technologies in areas like marketing, customer service, operations, and more. But the core message of this opening chapter is this: AI is for you, the small business owner. It's not some futuristic fantasy or exclusive club for big corporations. The AI revolution is happening on Main Street, and it's happening now. With the right mindset and the affordable tools now available, you can automate mundane tasks, scale your capabilities, and compete in the big leagues. Consider this an exciting new era – one where your creativity and entrepreneurial spirit, supercharged by AI, can take your business further than ever before. The playing field is leveling, the tools are democratized, and the advantage is yours to seize. So go ahead and take that first step into the world of AI-driven business – the frontier is wide open, and the potential rewards are vast.

Chapter 2

Building Your Small Business AI Advantage (Automate, Scale, Compete)

Every small business owner dreams of having an edge – a way to *automate* tedious tasks, *scale* operations, and *compete* with the giants without a Fortune 500 budget. The good news is that artificial intelligence is no longer just for big corporations with deep pockets. Today's AI tools are accessible, affordable, and user-friendly, meaning your local boutique or family restaurant can tap into the same kind of capabilities that industry leaders use. In fact, surveys show that 77% of small business professionals feel AI improves their work quality, and 75% believe it boosts their ability to compete with larger firms. By embracing AI strategically, you can *level the playing field* and create a "small business AI advantage" that propels your company forward. As one entrepreneur put it, "AI has de-stressed the workplace," freeing employees from drudgery to focus on more valuable work. This chapter will guide you through building that advantage step by step – from identifying what to automate first, to choosing the right low-cost tools, piloting projects on a budget, and measuring success so you can confidently scale up your efforts. Let's dive in with a conversational, can-do approach and see how even the smallest business can punch above its weight with AI.

Identifying High-Impact Automation Opportunities

Every successful AI implementation starts with a simple question: Where can it help the most? In a small business, resources are precious and time is money, so it's crucial to pinpoint the *high-impact pain points* – those routine tasks or bottlenecks that drain your time, money, or morale. Begin by evaluating your day-to-day operations. What tasks are your employees doing over and over? Where do errors often occur? Which processes make you sigh and think, "There's got to be a better way"? These areas are your best candidates for AI-driven improvement.

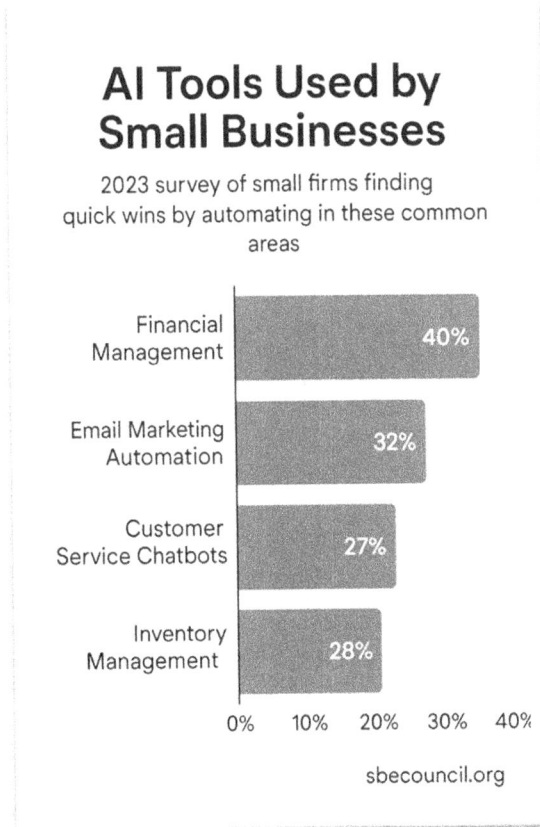

AI Tools Used by Small Businesses

2023 survey of small firms finding quick wins by automating in these common areas

Category	Percentage
Financial Management	40%
Email Marketing Automation	32%
Customer Service Chatbots	27%
Inventory Management	28%

0% 10% 20% 30% 40%

sbecouncil.org

Start by making a list of 3-5 tasks in your business that are repetitive, time-consuming, or prone to human error. For many, customer support jumps out as a pain point – maybe you're struggling to respond to inquiries fast enough, or you answer the same FAQs again and again. Perhaps data entry or invoice processing eats up hours that could be spent on strategy. Maybe inventory tracking is a headache – you're either running out of stock or drowning in excess because forecasting demand is tricky. Or it could be marketing outreach, like posting on social media daily or sending follow-up emails, which takes consistent effort. These are all ripe for AI automation. The key is to target tasks that *consume too much staff time or cause delays* in your operations. As you scan your workflow, ask: "If I could automate this, would it free me or my team to focus on higher-value activities?" If the answer is yes, put a star next to that item.

To illustrate, consider a few common scenarios. Imagine a small online retailer who finds that responding to customer questions is slowing down sales. Rather than hiring extra support staff, they deploy an AI chatbot on their website to answer common questions 24/7. Almost overnight, customers get instant answers about products and orders, and the business owner gains back hours previously spent glued to email. Now picture a family-run boutique that constantly struggles with inventory—some weeks they sell out of popular items too quickly, while other times they overstock and tie up cash in surplus goods. By tapping an AI-driven inventory forecasting tool, they can analyze sales patterns and predict demand, ensuring the right products are on the shelf at the right time. In the food industry, a local bakery might hate throwing away unsold cupcakes at day's end; with an AI system forecasting demand based on weather and past trends, they bake just enough and slash waste. And for a solo consultant or small consulting firm, researching client industries or compiling reports manually can take days – but using an AI assistant to gather data and even draft initial summaries can cut that research time dramatically, allowing them to serve more clients. In each case, the business identified a pain point that had an immediate impact on their bottom line (be it lost sales, wasted inventory, or hours of lost productivity) and flagged it as an AI opportunity.

Real-world examples bear this out. One UK-based retail SME, *Pampeano*, realized their inventory management was a competitive weakness. They deployed an AI tool to optimize stock levels and saw a noticeable increase in operational speed, which helped them compete against bigger retailers. Meanwhile, a small dress distributor named *Amarra* used AI to automate product descriptions and analyze sales data for demand predictions – as a result, they cut content creation time by 60% and reduced overstocking by 40%, directly saving time and money. These kinds of gains are transformative for a small business. The lesson is clear: by targeting the *right* problem – the one that causes the most pain – a little bit of AI can deliver an outsized benefit.

In practical terms, you might begin by rating potential automation projects on two scales: impact on the business (how much time/money it could save or new revenue it could generate) and feasibility (how straightforward it might be to implement). Prioritize something that scores high on impact and at least medium on feasibility. For example, automating your social media posting with an AI scheduling tool might be very feasible and save you a few hours a week – that's worth doing. But automating a complex, client-specific task might be lower feasibility for now. The goal is to find a quick win. Successful AI adoption often starts with a clearly defined use case where results will be visible quickly, building confidence for everyone involved. In summary, *think big, but start focused*: pick the low-hanging fruit first – those high-impact, tedious tasks that you'll be thrilled to hand over to an AI assistant.

Selecting the Right Low-Cost Tools and Platforms

Once you've identified *what* you want to automate or enhance with AI, the next question is *how* to do it – and specifically, how to do it without breaking the bank. The encouraging news is that not all AI solutions require a big budget or an in-house data scientist. In fact, there's an entire ecosystem of free and low-cost AI tools designed with small businesses in mind. This section is all about surveying the landscape of these tools and choosing the right one for your needs. The emphasis here is on practicality: affordable (often with free tiers), easy to use, and requiring little to no coding or technical expertise.

AI has been democratized. Thanks to cloud computing and clever software design, powerful AI capabilities are now available through simple apps or web platforms. You can sign up and start using many of these tools in minutes. For example, you no longer need a PhD in machine learning to deploy a customer service chatbot – services like Tidio or Drift let you plug a ready-made chatbot into your website by pasting a snippet of code. Need to generate marketing copy or social media posts? Tools like OpenAI's ChatGPT, Jasper, or Copy.ai can produce draft text for you; they often have free plans or trial periods to experiment. Want to forecast sales or analyze data? Even Microsoft Excel and Google Sheets have added AI-driven features (like automated data analysis) that a non-technical user can leverage, and there are lightweight analytics platforms offering predictive insights on a subscription model. The bottom line is you have options, and many of them are *either free or very low cost* to start.

Let's break down a few categories of AI tools that are especially relevant for small businesses, along with examples of affordable solutions in each category:

- Customer Service & Chatbots: These AI tools help you handle customer inquiries and support. Off-the-shelf chatbot platforms (e.g. Tidio, Freshdesk, or Drift) enable you to set up a website chat assistant that can answer FAQs, collect customer info, and even hand off to a human when needed. Many have free tiers that allow a certain number of conversations per month. Similarly, AI email assistants can draft responses to common customer emails. For instance, Gmail's built-in smart replies or third-party tools like Zoho Desk's AI can suggest replies to save you time. The goal is 24/7 responsiveness without hiring extra staff.

- Marketing & Sales Automation: This includes AI that helps with outreach, content creation, and sales processes. Email marketing platforms like Mailchimp and ActiveCampaign now have AI features that suggest the best times to send emails or even auto-generate email content tailored to different customer segments. Social media schedulers such as Buffer or Hootsuite use AI to recommend posting times or even craft captions. There are also AI-driven ad tools that optimize your Facebook or Google ads targeting. If you run an online store, AI recommendation engines (once only used by Amazon) are available as plugins to suggest products to your shoppers based on their browsing history. These solutions often cost a fraction of hiring a marketing agency – and in some cases, they're included in the software you may already use.

- Operations & Productivity: Think of the internal tasks – accounting, scheduling, document management – where AI can save you time. For example, bookkeeping software like QuickBooks now integrates AI to auto-categorize expenses or detect anomalies. If you dread scheduling appointments, AI scheduling assistants (like Calendly's more advanced features or Clara) can handle the back-and-forth of finding meeting times. For HR, tools like Breezy HR or Workable use AI to screen resumes faster. And don't overlook AI integrations in everyday tools: Microsoft's Power Platform and Google Workspace are adding AI copilots that draft documents, summarize meetings, and create presentations for you. These enterprise-grade features have trickled down to small biz packages, meaning you might already have some AI power at your fingertips without realizing it.

When selecting an AI tool, fit is everything. Here are some practical tips to ensure you choose the right solution for your business:

- Align with Your Needs: Look back at the high-impact area you identified. Make sure the tool actually addresses that problem. It sounds obvious, but with the buzz around AI, it's easy to get distracted by flashy tools that aren't what you need. Focus on the solution that solves *your* pain point – be it answering customer questions or forecasting inventory.

- Start with Free Trials: Most AI platforms offer a free tier or trial period. Take advantage of this. Before committing any money, sign up and test the tool in a real-world scenario. For instance, if you're eyeing an AI social media tool, use the free trial to schedule a week's posts and see how it goes. If it's a chatbot, run it on your site for a few days and see what customers ask it. This hands-on experience is invaluable.

- Read Reviews and Get Recommendations: Just as you might check Yelp before choosing a restaurant, check reviews on sites like Capterra, G2, or product forums. See what other small business users are saying. If you're part of any entrepreneur networking groups or online communities, ask around: *"Has anyone tried tool X for this? Would you recommend it?"* You'll often get candid insights. For example, a fellow small business owner might tell you that one AI scheduling app saved them 5 hours a week, while another had a clunky interface – that's good to know.

- **Ensure It Integrates:** Consider the tools you already use daily (your CRM, e-commerce platform, accounting software, etc.). Choosing an AI solution that *plays nicely* with your existing systems will save you headaches. Many low-cost AI tools have plugins or integrations for popular platforms. If not, you might be able to use automation services like Zapier as a bridge. The easier the integration, the quicker you get value.

- **Mind the Support and Learning Curve:** Even easy-to-use tools may require some learning. Check if the vendor offers tutorials, customer support, or an online knowledge base. Some of the best affordable tools have active user communities or support teams that can help you if you get stuck. You want to feel confident that if you encounter an issue, there's help available (even if it's just a good FAQ page or YouTube tutorials).

Above all, remember that *you don't need to spend a fortune to get started with AI.* Many small businesses dip their toes in with free versions and only scale up to paid plans once they see real results. Modern AI SaaS pricing is often pay-as-you-go or monthly subscription, so you can start small. As one 2025 report notes, accessible SaaS AI solutions have made advanced capabilities available without large upfront investments, essentially leveling the field for small firms. In short, pick a tool that fits your budget and skill level, and let it prove itself. If it delivers value, you can always expand usage or upgrade later – still at a fraction of the cost it would have taken to develop something in-house. With the right tool in hand, you're ready for the fun part: putting AI into action in your business.

Implementing on a Budget – Pilot Projects and Team Training

Adopting AI in a small business is best approached as a journey of *small steps* rather than a giant leap. Instead of overhauling everything at once (which can be risky, expensive, and overwhelming), you'll want to start with a pilot project – a limited, well-defined experiment to prove the concept. This strategy minimizes risk and cost, and it builds confidence within your team as you move forward. In this section, we outline a step-by-step game plan for rolling out AI on a budget: begin with one solution, integrate it into your workflow, train your team to use it, and create a culture that embraces innovation. Even with minimal resources, you'll see that *quick wins* are possible by starting small and then scaling up once you have proof that it works.

Step 1: Plan a Focused Pilot Project. Choose *one* AI initiative that addresses a high-impact area you identified. Define it clearly – for example, "implement an AI chatbot to handle live chat inquiries on our website," or "use an AI tool to automate our weekly sales reports." Keep the scope narrow enough that you can deploy it and evaluate results in a short timeframe (say, a few weeks to a couple of months). Research indicates that organizations taking a step-by-step approach with small pilots tend to have higher success rates than those attempting a "big bang" full implementation. The idea is to treat this like a trial run. Set specific goals for the pilot (e.g., reduce customer support response time by 50%, or save 5 hours per week on report generation). This will help you later determine if it's working.

Step 2: Get Buy-In and Involve Your Team Early. People are at the heart of any AI project – after all, your employees will be the ones using these tools day to day. It's crucial to bring them into the process from the beginning so they feel included rather than blindsided. Explain *why* you're introducing this AI solution and how it will help not just the business, but *make their work easier*. For instance, if you're rolling out an AI transcription tool to automatically take meeting notes, reassure the team that this isn't about cutting jobs – it's about freeing them from note-taking so they can focus on higher-level tasks. One key piece of advice is to show employees how the AI will support, not replace, their roles. In practical terms, you might hold a kickoff meeting or demo where you introduce the chosen tool, highlight its benefits, and invite questions. Employees who are engaged and feel heard are far more likely to embrace the new technology.

Step 3: Provide Training and Encourage Experimentation. Even user-friendly AI tools have a learning curve. Allocate some time to train the team members who will interact with the new system. This training doesn't have to be formal or costly – it could be as simple as a hands-on workshop or watching tutorial videos together. Many AI vendors offer free training resources or webinars; take advantage of those, and don't hesitate to use vendor support if available. Training is not a one-time event either. Encourage a culture of continuous learning and experimentation. Let your staff play around with the tool in a low-stakes environment (for example, set up a sandbox or test account where they can try it out without fear of messing up real data). When employees see that they can experiment and even make mistakes safely, they become more comfortable and might even discover creative new uses for the AI in your business. Crucially, by investing in your team's skills, you address one of the biggest barriers in AI adoption: the talent and knowledge gap. A recent survey found that while 86% of workers believed they'd need training in AI to keep up, only 14% had actually received any training so far. So, offering even a little training and practice puts you ahead of the curve in building an AI-ready team.

Step 4: Run the Pilot and Monitor Closely. Now comes the moment of truth – integrate the AI solution into your workflow on a small scale and let it run. During this pilot phase, keep a close eye on how things are going. Gather feedback from the team: Is the tool actually saving them time? Are there hiccups or frustrations? Also look at the data or metrics, if any, that the AI is affecting (we'll talk more about metrics in the next section, but even in a pilot you should have an eye on the key ones). The goal here is to learn, not to be perfect from day one. Maybe your new chatbot is great at answering 80% of questions but gets confused by the other 20% – that's useful insight. You can adjust its knowledge base or decide which questions should be routed to a human. Perhaps the AI inventory predictor is mostly accurate but missed an anomaly because you ran a big promotion that wasn't in the past data – that's an opportunity to learn and refine the model or settings. By testing in a controlled way, you can refine the approach before rolling it out more broadly. Think of it as a dress rehearsal for AI in your business.

Step 5: Celebrate Quick Wins and Address Challenges. As the pilot progresses, highlight any early successes. Did the pilot chatbot handle

200 customer questions in its first month? Share that with the team – it shows the value and builds momentum. If your AI tool booked 30 meetings without human intervention, that's a clear win. Celebrating these results boosts morale and reinforces why adopting AI was a good idea. At the same time, be transparent about challenges. If something isn't working as expected, involve the team in brainstorming solutions rather than quietly shelving the project. This openness contributes to an *innovation-friendly culture*, where people aren't afraid to try new things because they see that even if there are bumps in the road, the company will work through them constructively. For example, a professional services firm in one case introduced an AI scheduling assistant as a pilot. Within weeks, they cut appointment booking time by half and freed up staff for other work, giving them hard data to justify expanding the AI tool company-wide. On the other hand, a small legal firm that introduced AI transcription initially met resistance from paralegals worried about their jobs. But after a training session and a trial period, the staff realized the tool actually saved them hours of tedious work per week, and they enthusiastically embraced it. By piloting and addressing concerns through training and tweaks, that firm smoothed the adoption and set the stage for more innovation.

In summary, implementing AI on a budget is entirely feasible when you *start small and smart*. Involve your people, because fancy software means little without the team's buy-in and know-how. Leverage free resources for training and vendor support. Create a safe space for experimentation. And remember, even the most modest pilot project can score a meaningful win – a few hours saved, a few errors eliminated, a couple extra sales – that proves the value of AI to everyone. Once your pilot achieves those wins, you'll be ready to take the next step: measuring its impact in detail and deciding how to scale up further.

Measuring Success and Scaling Up

How do you know if your new AI chatbot or analytics tool is actually *moving the needle* for your business? One of the great advantages of digital tools is that they often come with data – and AI is no exception. To ensure that your AI initiatives truly benefit your bottom line (and to justify any further investment), you'll want to track specific metrics and establish feedback loops. This final section covers how to measure the success of your pilot (and subsequent projects) and how to use those results to improve and expand your AI usage over time. By being metrics-minded, even the most budget-conscious businesses can demonstrate ROI on AI and make informed decisions about scaling up.

Identify Key Performance Indicators (KPIs): Start by defining what success means for your AI project. This should tie back to the pain point you targeted. Common KPIs for AI projects include time saved, cost savings, error reduction, sales growth, lead conversion rate, customer satisfaction scores, and so on. For example, if you deployed an AI to automate customer support, you might measure average response time and customer satisfaction (perhaps through feedback or ratings). If it's an inventory AI, you might track stockout incidents (hoping they decrease) and inventory carrying cost savings. A marketing AI might be evaluated on increase in leads or web traffic. The key is to pick metrics that directly reflect the improvement you hope to see. Be as concrete as possible: e.g., "reduce data entry errors by 90%" or "save 10 hours per week on accounting tasks." Having these targets allows you to objectively evaluate the AI's impact. As one expert noted, setting measurable objectives (like *reduced processing time by X%* or *improved lead conversion by Y%*) ensures that each AI initiative is tied to a real business goal.

Track and Compare: Once the AI is in action, start collecting data on those KPIs. It's often helpful to have a "before AI" baseline for comparison. If your average customer email response time was 4 hours before the chatbot, and now it's 1 hour with the chatbot, that's a clear improvement. If you used to spend 5 hours a week scheduling appointments and now the AI does it in 30 minutes, you just saved nearly a full workday. Quantify these changes. Many small businesses find that AI tools deliver surprisingly tangible results. For instance, one small consulting firm using an AI-driven CRM to automate follow-ups saw a 30% increase in closed deals within six months – a metric that directly translated to revenue growth. A boutique marketing agency that started using AI for content creation was able to produce 40% more content (and serve more clients) without adding headcount. These are the kinds of outcomes you want to capture in your metrics. They tell a story: AI freed up X hours, or AI boosted output by Y%, etc. Not every metric will be a home run, of course. Some might show modest changes or even no improvement if the tool isn't used optimally yet. That's fine – the point of measurement is to learn and adjust.

Gather Qualitative Feedback: Numbers are important, but don't ignore the qualitative side. Talk to your team and even customers about the AI's impact. Are employees less stressed because tedious tasks are off their plate? Do they report having more time to focus on creative or strategic work? Are customers happier with faster service or more personalized attention? Sometimes a quote or anecdote can highlight value that's hard to capture in a spreadsheet. For example, maybe your customer support rep mentions, "Since the chatbot handles the easy questions, my day is so much smoother and I can spend extra time solving the tough cases for customers." That indicates higher quality service and perhaps improved employee morale. Or a customer says, "Love the new instant chat on your site!" – a good sign you're gaining loyalty. This kind of feedback can supplement the hard data and give you a fuller picture of success.

Refine and Improve: Measurement isn't just about patting yourself on the back for wins – it's about spotting areas to improve. If your AI isn't hitting the targets you set, dig into why. Do you need to tweak the tool's settings or provide more training to staff on using it? Perhaps the data feeding the AI needs cleaning or updating (garbage in, garbage out, as the saying goes). Treat the initial deployment as version 1.0. Use what you learn to refine the process. Maybe you discover that your AI marketing tool performs great on Facebook but poorly on email content – so you adjust your strategy to use it more on the channel where it excels. Or you find employees aren't using the tool as much as expected; maybe they need a refresher training or a clearer mandate on when to use it. Continuous improvement is the name of the game. As one business advisor aptly put it, AI is not a set-it-and-forget-it solution – you should regularly assess if the tool is meeting your goals and make adjustments as needed. The experience of a family-run hotel offers a great example: they set up an AI chatbot for guest inquiries and after three months, noticed some guests were frustrated with the automated responses. The team reviewed the transcripts, tweaked the bot's scripts and added an easy option to reach a human. The result? Guest satisfaction went up again. This kind of iterative tweaking is normal and expected; the insight you gain from real usage is what guides the improvements.

Deciding When to Scale Up: If your pilot project is knocking it out of the park – or even just delivering a solid benefit – you'll likely start asking: what next? Scaling up can mean expanding the AI solution to more users, more departments, or into other processes. For example, if the chatbot for customer service worked well, maybe next you deploy a similar chatbot on your Facebook page, or you extend it to handle some basic sales inquiries as well. If the AI inventory tool was a success in one product line, you might roll it out across all your product categories. The decision to scale should be based on both the quantitative ROI and your company's readiness. You'll need to ensure you have the budget for any increased usage costs and that your team is prepared to manage a broader implementation. Often, the data from your pilot makes a strong case: if you can show that *"AI saved us $X or generated $Y in this trial run,"* it becomes much easier to justify further investment. Many small businesses find that the time savings alone are worth it – one estimate suggested that across U.S. small businesses, AI could save around 6.3 billion hours of labor, equating to about $273 billion in savings annually if extrapolated. Your individual business might only save a slice of that pie, but even a few thousand dollars' worth of time can be significant for a small operation.

When scaling up, do so responsibly and mindfully. It can be tempting to rush into deploying AI everywhere once you see a success, but maintain the same thoughtful approach you used for the pilot. Continue to monitor performance closely as you expand. Keep setting KPIs for new areas you implement AI. Also, ensure that the human element stays in focus – maintain transparency with employees about new changes, continue to get their input, and watch out for "AI overload" (introducing too many new tools at once can overwhelm people). It's often wise to scale in phases: add one new function or department at a time, rather than five at once, so you can manage the transition smoothly.

Finally, foster a culture of continuous improvement and learning. AI technology evolves quickly – new features, better algorithms, and entirely new tools are coming out all the time. Encourage your team to stay curious and up-to-date. Perhaps schedule a review every 3-6 months to revisit your AI tools: Are there updates we should adopt? Any new solutions in the market that address our next pain point? By keeping an eye on the horizon, you ensure that your "small business AI advantage" grows over time rather than stagnates. Remember, the aim is not to implement AI for AI's sake, but to build a smarter, more efficient, and competitive business. If you measure what matters and scale deliberately, you'll be well on your way to doing just that.

Real-World Wrap-Up: By tracking results and iterating, many small businesses have turned modest AI experiments into game-changing transformations. We've mentioned how a consulting firm boosted sales follow-ups by 30% and a retailer saved hours with a chatbot – those companies didn't stop there. They used those wins to justify AI in other areas, gradually scaling up until AI became an integral part of their operations. The result is often a business that can *do more with less*: serve more customers, analyze more data, and work smarter than ever before. And perhaps the best part for a small business owner? You gain confidence that you can compete with the big players. When you see your customer satisfaction rising or your costs falling, it validates that these new technologies are truly an equalizer. By measuring outcomes and scaling up thoughtfully, you ensure that AI continues to work for you, not the other way around. Your small business can then fully leverage the AI advantage – automating, scaling, and competing in ways that were once the exclusive domain of Fortune 500 companies, but are now within your reach.

Chapter 3

AI in Retail – Modernizing the Small Shop Experience

rtificial Intelligence is revolutionizing the way small retailers do business. Not long ago, many advanced retail technologies – from personalized shopping recommendations to dynamic pricing algorithms – were exclusive to industry giants with deep pockets. Today, however, even the smallest boutique or corner shop can leverage affordable AI tools to automate and enhance their operations, bridging the gap and competing with much larger companies. In this chapter, we explore how AI is modernizing the small shop experience in four key areas: by enabling personalized customer engagement, smart inventory management, targeted marketing with dynamic pricing, and by showcasing a real-world case study of a boutique retailer that thrived using AI. Each section illustrates how free or low-cost AI solutions can empower small businesses to deliver concierge-level service, optimize their stock, and make data-driven decisions – ultimately helping them scale up and compete with Fortune 500 retailers.

Personalized Customer Engagement and Service

One of the most visible ways AI is transforming retail is by allowing small businesses to offer personalized, concierge-level customer service at scale. In a traditional shop, a great sales associate remembers regular customers' preferences and can make tailored recommendations. AI now enables even a tiny online store or local boutique to achieve a similar personal touch for every customer. Through tools like AI chatbots and recommender systems, a small retailer can make each shopper feel recognized and catered to, much like having a personal shopping assistant available at all times.

AI-Powered Chatbots for 24/7 Service

An AI chatbot on a retail website can instantly handle customer inquiries and provide friendly service around the clock – something that used to require hiring staff for overnight shifts. For example, a small boutique might deploy a chatbot to answer questions about product availability, sizing, or store policies at any hour. Customers visiting the boutique's site could ask, "Do you have this jacket in a size M?" and the AI assistant would immediately check inventory and respond, or explain the return policy if asked. Such a system ensures shoppers get the information they need without delay, greatly improving convenience. In fact, one local boutique that added an AI chatbot was able to offer 24/7 customer support, instantly answering questions about products and policies and freeing up their human staff to focus on in-store shoppers. Modern AI chatbots leverage Natural Language Processing (NLP) to understand queries and can handle everything from FAQs to order tracking and returns. These bots reply within seconds and never need a break, enabling a small business to field customer questions *around the clock* without a large support team. Impressively, a well-designed chatbot can even make product suggestions based on what a customer is asking or browsing, functioning like a virtual sales associate. By removing the need for human intervention, AI chatbots let a small retailer provide high-quality customer care at any hour – but without the usual costs of maintaining a full staff.

Personalized Product Recommendations

Beyond answering questions, AI enables *personalized product recommendations* that rival the "customers also liked" features of major e-commerce sites. Recommender systems analyze each shopper's browsing and purchase history to learn their tastes and predict what they might want next. Even a tiny online shop can implement recommendation algorithms (often available as plugins or affordable services) to showcase items uniquely suited to each visitor. For instance, if an online boutique notices a customer frequently buys vintage-style dresses, an AI engine can highlight new arrivals in that style or suggest matching accessories. These tailored recommendations make customers feel understood and often lead to additional sales. Studies have shown that AI-driven recommendation engines can significantly boost conversion rates and average order value – by as much as 30% and 50%, respectively – simply by presenting shoppers with relevant items they are likely to buy. This kind of personalization was once the domain of retail giants with dedicated data science teams, but now accessible AI tools let small businesses achieve it too. By leveraging customers' data ethically and intelligently, a boutique can mimic the personal shopper experience: "We thought you'd love this new item," or "Since you bought those shoes, here's a handbag that would go perfectly." Shoppers are delighted by the serendipity of finding products that match their style, which increases their satisfaction and loyalty to the store.

Ultimately, personalized engagement through AI – whether via friendly chatbots or smart recommendations – helps a small retailer punch above its weight in customer service. Shoppers feel *seen* and valued because the business remembers their needs and preferences. This drives higher satisfaction and fosters loyalty, as buyers return to the place that "just gets" their tastes. By making every customer feel attended to individually, a small shop can build stronger relationships than ever before, translating into repeat business and positive word-of-mouth. AI gives even the smallest retail business the power to treat each customer like a VIP, creating a modernized shopping experience that keeps people coming back.

Smart Inventory Management and Supply Chain Optimization

Stocking the right products at the right time is a perpetual challenge for retailers. For a small shop, every inch of storage and every dollar tied up in inventory counts – yet running out of a popular item means a lost sale and a disappointed customer. Traditionally, small retailers had to rely on spreadsheets, intuition, or last year's sales data to guess how much to stock, often resulting in overstocked shelves of slow sellers or empty racks where the best-sellers should be. Now, AI-driven predictive analytics is changing the game, helping even modest businesses forecast demand and manage inventory with unprecedented precision. In fact, nearly half of businesses (48%) now leverage technologies like predictive analytics and machine learning to make data-driven inventory decisions – a trend that is truly leveling the playing field between small shops and big chains.

AI Demand Forecasting

Predictive analytics software can analyze a wide range of data – past sales records, seasonal buying patterns, holiday spikes, and even external factors – to accurately forecast what products will sell, when, and in what quantity. Modern AI systems don't just look at yesterday's sales; they can incorporate data like local weather forecasts, social media trends, or nearby events to anticipate changes in demand. For example, if a cold front is coming, an AI system for a clothing boutique might predict increased demand for jackets and scarves and suggest stocking up accordingly. By crunching such data, AI can alert a shop owner that, say, demand for green widgets will likely double next month, or that floral dresses will be trendy this spring based on social buzz – so they can order sufficient stock in advance. The result is that small retailers using these tools can avoid the classic pitfalls of inventory management. They won't overstock items that won't sell (tying up cash in surplus inventory), and they won't miss out on sales by understocking hot items. As one AI platform vendor explained, this approach "translates to enhanced efficiency, less cost, and greater customer satisfaction" because stores are far less likely to be out of what customers want.

Optimizing Stock Levels and Reducing Waste

By forecasting more accurately, AI helps business owners maintain optimal stock levels at all times. Instead of a backroom full of dusty clearance items, the inventory more closely matches real customer demand. This leads to less waste (fewer unsold products that must be discounted or thrown out) and fewer "sorry, we're out of that item" moments. In practice, small retailers are seeing tangible benefits. Nearly every time a product is out-of-stock is a missed revenue opportunity – but AI is helping to eliminate those. One case study found that adopting AI-based inventory management led to significantly fewer stockouts and overstock situations. For instance, an emerging fashion retailer that implemented an AI forecasting tool experienced a major decrease in stockouts during peak seasons and was able to cut down on over-ordering, thereby reducing wasteful excess inventory. Customers of that store noticed the difference – their favorite items were more reliably available, which boosted the store's reputation for consistency.

Reliability and Customer Satisfaction

Smart inventory optimization doesn't just save money; it also delights customers. When shoppers can trust that your small shop will have the products they want in stock, they're more likely to return and recommend your business to others. Conversely, nothing erodes customer goodwill faster than empty shelves or long waits for restocks. By using AI to get inventory right, a boutique can essentially never miss a sale due to stockouts while also avoiding the waste of overstock. Moreover, AI can help streamline the supply chain as well – for instance, by automatically reordering popular products before they run out, or by flagging potential supplier issues in advance. An intelligent system might even predict a looming supply chain disruption (say a shipping delay or a supplier shortfall) by analyzing data patterns, giving the business a chance to adapt proactively. This reliability becomes a competitive advantage. In an era where nearly half of retailers are using predictive analytics, small businesses that adopt these tools signal to customers that they are just as data-savvy and dependable as the retail giants. They enjoy the dual benefits of saving costs (by not overstocking) and increasing revenue (by always having the in-demand items ready to go). In short, AI-powered inventory management takes much of the guesswork out of stocking a small shop, allowing owners to make informed decisions that keep their business lean, efficient, and ready to serve customers with exactly what they're looking for.

Targeted Marketing and Dynamic Pricing Strategies

Being able to **market smarter** and react swiftly to market changes is another advantage AI hands to small retailers. In the past, sophisticated customer analytics and real-time pricing adjustments were luxuries that only big retail chains could deploy. Now, AI-driven services make these capabilities available to businesses of any size, allowing a small retailer to reach the right customers with the right message – and to set the right price at the right time – far more efficiently than traditional methods.

AI-Driven Targeted Marketing

Small retailers typically can't afford huge blanket advertising campaigns, so their marketing needs to be precise and cost-effective. AI analytics provide exactly that edge: by analyzing customer data, AI can segment a retailer's customer base into meaningful groups and help tailor promotions for each segment. Instead of sending out one-size-fits-all flyers or emails, a boutique can use AI to identify who is most likely to buy a particular product and target those people with a personalized offer. For example, an AI tool might analyze purchase history and discover that a group of customers regularly buys eco-friendly products – the shop could then send them a special "green products" newsletter or discount code relevant to their interests. This kind of focused marketing ensures that promotional efforts reach those most likely to buy, often at a fraction of the cost of broad advertising. As one source noted, AI allows small businesses to "reach the right people with the right message" and run successful campaigns for far fewer dollars than old-school mass marketing. AI-driven marketing platforms can automatically manage tasks like sending personalized emails, launching social media ads, and even choosing the optimal time to post or send messages for maximum engagement. Moreover, AI can continuously analyze campaign performance in real time, fine-tuning the approach to improve results. A process that once took weeks of guessing and manual analysis can now happen in hours, as algorithms test different content and timing to see what works best. This data-driven approach gives small retailers a marketing advantage by squeezing more results out of a modest budget

– effectively letting them punch above their weight in attracting and retaining customers.

Dynamic Pricing for Competitiveness

Just as AI helps target the right customers, it also helps small retailers set prices strategically in response to market conditions. Large e-commerce players famously adjust their prices multiple times a day based on supply and demand, but today even a neighborhood store can utilize dynamic pricing tools to stay competitive. AI-powered pricing systems monitor factors like competitor pricing, demand fluctuations, and inventory levels, then recommend (or automatically implement) price adjustments on the fly. For instance, if a competing shop across town or an online rival discounts a certain product, an AI system could alert a small retailer to adjust their own price to match – or to emphasize a different value proposition if undercutting the competitor isn't feasible. Similarly, if a particular item is selling faster than expected, AI might suggest a slight price increase to maximize margins without significantly hurting sales. On the flip side, for slow-moving stock, the system could propose timely markdowns or promotions to stimulate demand. In short, dynamic pricing algorithms give small businesses a level of agility in pricing that was once the domain of Amazon-like giants. As one platform provider explains, AI tools can continuously compare a small shop's prices against market trends and competitors, enabling real-time price tweaks that keep the store's offerings attractive yet profitable. Importantly, these pricing optimizations don't mean racing to the bottom – the goal is to find the sweet spot where prices are competitive but still sustain a healthy margin. In fact, industry research predicts that adopting AI-driven dynamic pricing can increase a retailer's revenue by up to 3% and boost profit margins by as much as 10% through intelligent real-time adjustments. Those percentage gains can make a significant difference for a small business's bottom line.

What's remarkable is that strategies like personalized marketing campaigns and dynamic pricing – once available only to firms with advanced IT and analytics departments – are now within reach for independent retailers. A variety of accessible AI platforms and services (often offered on a subscription model or even with free tiers) can handle the heavy lifting. For example, services like Nector.io provide small businesses with AI-driven pricing and marketing solutions that keep their prices competitive without "burning margins," meaning a shop can respond to market changes without sacrificing profitability. By leveraging such tools, a boutique or family-run store can react to customer trends and competitive moves in real time, just like a Fortune 500 retailer. The end result is a more dynamic and resilient business – one that can seize opportunities (or mitigate challenges) as they arise. With AI in their toolkit, small retailers can market and price their products with a new level of sophistication, winning customers' attention and loyalty while still protecting their bottom line.

Case Study – Boutique Retailer Thrives with AI: TrendThreads

All of the above concepts come together in the story of TrendThreads, a small specialty clothing boutique that achieved remarkable results by embracing AI. TrendThreads wanted to better understand its customers and compete with larger fashion retailers, so it turned to an AI-driven analytics platform to make sense of its data. The system analyzed each customer's purchase history and online browsing behavior, allowing TrendThreads to build detailed profiles for everyone who shopped with them. Armed with these insights, the boutique crafted highly personalized marketing outreach – for example, sending tailored email campaigns and targeted promotions featuring items that each customer would likely be interested in. If one shopper often bought vintage denim, their emails showcased the latest vintage-style jeans; if another preferred bohemian dresses, they'd receive lookbooks and discounts for the new boho-chic arrivals. This individualized approach made customers feel understood and catered to, leading to a notable boost in engagement and repeat sales for the store. In other words, TrendThreads used AI to give every customer the kind of personal attention that builds loyalty.

At the same time, TrendThreads applied AI to its operations, particularly inventory management. The boutique used AI-based demand forecasting to accurately predict which styles and sizes would be popular in upcoming seasons. By analyzing sales trends and even browsing data (like how many people clicked on a coming-soon item), the AI could forecast demand for each product and recommend optimal stock levels. Thanks to this, TrendThreads was able to optimize its inventory – ordering the right amounts of each item and timing restocks perfectly. The store drastically reduced the risk of running out of hot sellers, and it also avoided overstocking items that wouldn't move. The results were quickly apparent: the shop never had to turn eager customers away due to an item being out-of-stock, and it cut down on wasted inventory that sat unsold. By always having the "in" products available when customers wanted them, TrendThreads not only saved money but also delighted shoppers with its reliability. The AI forecasts even helped streamline the boutique's supply chain coordination, ensuring new inventory arrived just as it was needed.

The success of TrendThreads demonstrates that the right AI tools can indeed empower a small retailer to compete with far larger competitors. By leveraging customer analytics and predictive forecasting, this boutique achieved gains in both customer loyalty and sales that might have once seemed out of reach for a business of its size. Shoppers started to treat TrendThreads with the same enthusiasm and trust they'd give to a big-brand store – because the boutique could cater to their tastes and keep the items they loved in stock. In essence, AI allowed TrendThreads to scale the quality of its customer experience and operations without losing its personal, small-shop charm. For any small business owner, TrendThreads is a compelling example of how adopting accessible AI solutions can translate into increased customer loyalty and revenue. It's proof that even a modest boutique can thrive in the modern retail landscape when it harnesses the power of AI. The playing field between the corner store and the Fortune 500 retailer is more level than ever – and AI is a big reason why.

Chapter 4

AI in Consulting and Professional Services – Amplifying Your Expertise

Small consulting firms and professional service providers are discovering that artificial intelligence (AI) can dramatically amplify their expertise. In an industry long dominated by big firms with vast resources, AI is helping level the playing field for small players. With the right free or low-cost AI tools, even a boutique consultancy can *compete on equal footing* – delivering insights and service quality once reserved for Fortune 500–level firms. In this chapter, we explore how AI accelerates research, automates routine tasks, enhances client engagement, and ultimately transforms a small firm's capabilities. The tone is practical and inspirational: AI isn't about replacing the human touch, but amplifying your expertise so you can automate, scale, and thrive.

Accelerating Research and Data Analysis

For many small consultancies – from management advisors to accountants and legal practitioners – intensive research and data analysis are daily challenges. Limited staff means a single person might spend days sifting through industry reports, survey results, or financial data to find actionable insights. Here's where AI shines as a tireless junior analyst. Modern AI tools can ingest and analyze vast amounts of information at lightning speed, identifying patterns or red flags that inform client strategies in a fraction of the time a human would need.

AI as a "junior analyst." Imagine having an assistant who can read thousands of survey responses or pages of market research in minutes, highlighting trends and anomalies. AI-driven analytics platforms offer exactly that capability. They use machine learning and natural language processing to comb through unstructured data (like customer feedback or social media comments) as well as structured datasets (like sales figures or financial statements). The AI can then surface key findings – for example, "customers in region X report rising demand for product Y," or "Q3 expenses exceeded the benchmark by 15% in these categories." Armed with these insights, the human consultant can focus on interpreting the *why* and *how* for the client, rather than spending all their time on the initial number-crunching.

Crucially, AI doesn't just work faster – it can also go deeper. Advanced analytics that were once the secret weapon of large firms are now accessible to small businesses. AI tools today enable even a solo consultant to process vast data and generate high-quality, data-driven recommendations in real time. This means you can extract insights from big data sets that previously would have required a dedicated team of analysts. One white paper notes that AI has effectively eliminated the traditional knowledge gap between large firms (with extensive research departments) and smaller firms with limited resources. A small outfit can now draw on the *same level of data analysis and predictive capability* as a top-tier consulting house, using affordable AI platforms.

Finding patterns humans might miss. AI is exceptionally good at pattern recognition. For example, let's say your consulting project involves analyzing a client's customer survey data. Manually, you might sample responses or use basic spreadsheet functions; an AI, however, can parse every single response and perform sentiment analysis, cluster common themes, and correlate feedback with customer demographics *within seconds*. By integrating AI into survey data analysis, a small firm can uncover hidden trends without hiring extra analysts or outsourcing the job. In fact, AI survey tools have been shown to cut analysis costs dramatically – one comparison found that analyzing a dataset of 1,000 survey responses plus preparing a report could cost a small business around $640 manually, but only about $180 with AI assistance. The AI not only saves money but also frees up human consultants from hours of tedious work. The *result*: insights arrive faster, and consultants can redirect their time to higher-level thinking.

Consider a real example: A boutique management consultant working for a mid-sized logistics company used AI to analyze the client's supply chain data and customer trends. Thanks to AI, this solo consultant delivered the *same depth of insight* as a large firm's entire analysis team – and did it faster and at a fraction of the cost. The AI sifted through years of supply chain records and market forecasts to pinpoint inefficiencies and opportunities. Armed with these findings, the consultant proposed strategic changes that saved the client money and improved delivery times. This kind of rapid, data-backed insight would have been hard to achieve before, but AI made it possible for a small firm to shine.

From big data to actionable advice. AI doesn't just accelerate number-crunching; it helps translate data into decisions. Sophisticated tools can generate visualizations, write summaries, or even draft initial recommendations based on the patterns they detect. For instance, an AI might analyze a client's financial reports and automatically flag that *"marketing ROI has been declining quarter-over-quarter while customer acquisition cost is rising"*. The consultant can take that alert and investigate further, then advise on a strategy (maybe reallocate the marketing budget or target a different customer segment). One case study described how after implementing AI for data analysis, a consulting firm began uncovering business insights that would have been hard to see before – the AI found subtle trends in customer behavior that the human team hadn't noticed, enabling more informed strategic advice. In effect, AI acts as an extra pair of eyes, ensuring nothing important in the data goes unnoticed.

What's more, AI has democratized access to knowledge that used to be the privilege of big enterprises. Large consulting companies often had subscriptions to expensive databases or proprietary research – advantages out of reach for small firms. Today, many AI systems pull from publicly available information, industry databases, and real-time web data to give any consultant a rich informational foundation. Powerful language models can summarize industry news, analyst reports, or even academic papers on demand. For example, an independent financial consultant can use natural language processing tools to extract key insights from vast sources – investor presentations, economic forecasts, industry analyses – without a research team or pricey reports. The AI continuously learns and updates with the latest data, so you're always working with current information, not last year's intel. This means a small firm can walk into a client meeting armed with up-to-the-minute industry insights, just like a Fortune 500 consultant would.

Speed and depth rivaling larger firms. By letting AI handle the heavy lifting of research, small firms can provide data-backed recommendations with a speed and thoroughness that *rivals far larger competitors*. One consultant put it this way: "99.9% of businesses could never afford McKinsey or any of the MBB firms. We created an AI so anyone could have the power of a consulting firm at their hands when they need it.". This quote, from the cofounder of an AI strategy platform, underscores the new reality – advanced business analysis is no longer the exclusive domain of mega-firms. Tools like that AI strategy chatbot (which can produce deliverables such as a detailed 60-page business plan or market strategy) demonstrate how even complex consulting outputs can be generated quickly by AI. Of course, human expertise is still crucial to refine and contextualize these outputs, but the first draft or initial analysis can be done in minutes, not weeks.

In summary, AI is supercharging research and analysis for small professional service firms. It acts as a force multiplier for your knowledge and skills. You can tackle projects that used to be beyond your bandwidth, confident that AI will surface critical insights and patterns. This not only improves the quality of your work but also impresses clients – they see a smaller firm delivering insight with the speed and depth they'd expect from a big name consultancy. And as a bonus, the efficiency gains mean you can handle more projects or spend more time on creative problem-solving, rather than drowning in data. The playing field is truly leveling: *"AI tools now enable smaller firms and individual consultants to compete on a more equal footing, delivering the same quality of insights and services that previously only big firms could provide."*

Automating Administrative and Routine Tasks

In small professional service firms, it's common for team members to wear many hats. You might be the advisor or expert one moment, and the office administrator, scheduler, and bookkeeper the next. These routine tasks – while essential – can eat up hours of your day. The more time you spend on scheduling meetings, inputting data, processing invoices, or drafting form letters, the less time you have for high-value consulting work. This is where AI becomes a powerful ally: it can take over many of those administrative burdens, *freeing you up to focus on your specialized expertise.*

The burden of "many hats." As one legal tech blog noted, when you're simultaneously the lawyer, office manager, and IT support, routine tasks can devour the hours you need for client work. This scenario applies to any small firm – whether you're a consultant, accountant, or marketing freelancer, you've likely felt the pinch of having more tasks than time. AI tools can step in to handle lots of repetitive jobs, operating like a tireless assistant working in the background. The result is not just time saved, but also reduced stress and fewer things "falling through the cracks" when you're juggling too much.

Let's break down a few examples of administrative or routine tasks that AI can automate for you:

- Appointment scheduling and calendar management: Instead of the back-and-forth emails to set up client calls or meetings, AI-driven schedulers can do it automatically. For instance, Motion's AI Meeting Assistant and similar tools can coordinate availability and book meetings via email or a web link without your manual involvement. You simply set your preferences, and the AI handles the rest – proposing times, sending invites, even rescheduling if needed. Some AI scheduling assistants (formerly tools like x.ai's Amy or newer calendar AI integrations) operate almost like a virtual secretary, engaging in natural email conversation with your clients to finalize a meeting time. The benefit is twofold: you reclaim hours of your week, and clients get prompt, 24/7 service in booking time with you. In fact, modern client intake platforms use AI to qualify leads and schedule appointments around the clock, ensuring potential clients are attended to even if you're busy or asleep. No more missed opportunities because you didn't reply fast enough – the AI has your calendar covered.

- Data entry and invoice processing: Few things are more tedious than transferring data from one system to another or manually entering figures from receipts. AI can handle these mind-numbing tasks with higher speed and accuracy. For example, accounting firms now use AI-powered software to automatically extract information from invoices, receipts, and financial statements, then populate that data into spreadsheets or accounting systems. This means an invoice that used to be hand-keyed by an admin can be scanned by an AI vision tool; within seconds, the AI captures the vendor name, date, line items, amounts, etc., and updates your records. Not only does this minimize manual effort and reduce errors, it also accelerates processes like bookkeeping and tax preparation. Even if you're not an accountant, think of parallel examples: an HR consultant could use AI to parse resumes into a database, or a legal practitioner could deploy AI to sort and file digital documents by reading their contents. In a nutshell, any repetitive task that follows rules or patterns is a good candidate for AI automation. The upshot is you can handle the administrative load without hiring additional staff, which is crucial when budgets are tight.

- Organizing and managing documents: Professional services generate tons of documents – case files, research notes, proposals, contracts, emails. Keeping these organized is a chore that AI can help simplify. For example, in a small law office, an AI tool like Clio's document assistant can automatically categorize case documents, flag important clauses, and even summarize long contracts for quicker review. Instead of an attorney or paralegal spending hours skimming and organizing PDFs, the AI reads through them and identifies what's key (e.g. deadlines, obligations, unusual terms). Similarly, a management consultant could use an AI to digest lengthy client reports or industry regulations, pulling out the pieces that matter. Think of it as having a smart file clerk who not only files documents but actually understands them and briefs you on the content. This intelligent organization means you can retrieve information faster and ensure nothing critical is overlooked in the paperwork deluge.

- Drafting routine communications and reports: Composing the first draft of a document is often the most time-consuming part. AI writing assistants can generate initial drafts of standard documents so you're never starting from a blank page. Need a draft of a consulting engagement letter, a project proposal, or a follow-up email? Provide a few key details to an AI (or use a template as a prompt), and it will produce a coherent draft in seconds. For instance, AI proposal generators have matured to the point where they *automatically generate content and tailor documents to specific client requirements,* organizing the text and even suggesting data points to include. These tools can save you significant time on proposals – one source notes they help teams quickly produce well-researched, persuasive proposals, freeing up time for other work. The AI ensures the formatting is tidy and the language is professional, reducing the chance of human error in your rush to meet a deadline. After the AI's first pass, you simply review and fine-tune the document to add your personal touch or specialized insight. The result is a polished deliverable prepared in a fraction of the usual time.

- Email follow-ups and personalized outreach: Keeping up with client communications is vital, but crafting individualized follow-up emails after meetings or sales calls can be repetitive. AI can help here as well. Integrated with your Customer Relationship

Management (CRM) system, AI can draft and even send follow-up emails that *feel* personal. It might pull in key points from your last meeting notes ("It was great discussing your expansion plans in our call yesterday…") and combine it with known client preferences to compose a tailored message. Modern AI-enabled CRMs actually analyze customer interactions and can automate personalized follow-ups and email sequences with minimal effort. For example, one business tech article highlights that AI can handle scheduling of follow-up emails and sending reminders, which frees small business owners from having to remember every single touchpoint. The AI ensures consistency – no client slips through the cracks due to forgetfulness – and it can optimize timing (sending emails at the time of day each client is most likely to engage). Importantly, these messages can be more than canned templates; with AI's language generation, they can incorporate details that make each email genuinely relevant to the recipient. This kind of automation lets a solo consultant maintain a high level of professional communication that rivals a larger firm's CRM-driven outreach, *without hiring a full-time assistant or marketing team.*

By delegating routine tasks to intelligent assistants, small firms can dramatically increase their operational efficiency. A telling example comes from the legal field: lawyers often struggle with being attorney, receptionist, and bookkeeper all at once. AI tools for small law firms now handle tasks like client intake, appointment booking, document drafting, even tracking billable time – essentially acting as a digital paralegal and secretary. As a result, lawyers free up hours to actually practice law and serve clients. The same principle applies across consulting and professional services. When AI shoulders the repetitive work, you regain capacity to do what you do best (whether that's giving strategic advice, building relationships, or creative problem solving).

Moreover, leveraging AI for admin tasks can make a tiny firm appear "bigger" and more capable to clients. With prompt responses, organized processes, and polished documents, clients will feel like you have a whole support staff – even if it's really just you and your AI helpers behind the scenes. For example, an AI chatbot on your website can instantly answer common client questions or help them schedule a call, providing immediate service that would typically require a dedicated client coordinator. It's not about fooling anyone; it's about delivering service quality on par with large firms. One entrepreneur observed that many internal processes at consulting firms "lend themselves almost perfectly" to what generative AI can do. So, small firms that embrace these AI-driven processes can streamline operations and respond faster than competitors bogged down by manual work. In fact, some emerging AI platforms specifically aim to make *small consultancies more competitive by automating tedious processes like proposal writing and research* – thereby reducing bureaucracy and boosting responsiveness.

In short, AI automation lets you punch above your weight class. You can maintain lean operations (keeping overhead low) while still handling a high volume of work with quality and consistency. The mundane chores that used to consume evenings or weekends become automated tasks you only supervise occasionally. This not only boosts productivity and reduces burnout, but also creates a better experience for clients (who receive quicker turnaround and fewer errors). When you're both the brain (expert) and the brawn (administration) of your business, having AI take over the "brawn" duties is a game-changer.

Enhancing Client Engagement and Value Delivery

Beyond efficiency and cost savings, AI offers small consulting and service firms a way to deliver a superior client experience and more value. In today's market, clients expect high-touch service – *rapid responses, personalized attention, and data-informed insights* – regardless of a firm's size. Meeting these expectations can strain a small team, but AI tools can bridge the gap by augmenting how you engage and serve your clients. Here we look at how AI can help a nimble firm feel to the client like an extended, always-available team that's proactive and informed.

Responsive and available service. Clients love quick answers and support when they need it. AI enables a level of responsiveness that would be hard to maintain manually in a small firm. A prime example is deploying AI-powered chatbots or virtual assistants on your website or messaging platforms. These bots can handle common inquiries 24/7, providing instant answers about your services, scheduling, or basic troubleshooting. That means a potential client browsing your site at 10 PM can get their questions answered immediately ("Do you offer X service?", "How do I book a consultation?") rather than waiting days for an email reply. Small businesses have successfully used such chatbots to boost customer satisfaction – one retail shop implemented an AI chatbot for FAQs and saw a 30% increase in online sales because customers found the instant answers increased their trust and convenience. For a consulting firm, while the outcome might not be online sales, the impact is similar: clients feel cared for at all times, and your team is freed from handling repetitive queries. The chatbot essentially triages client needs, resolving the simple ones and passing on only the complex issues to you. This not only reduces wait times and ensures no inquiry slips through, but also lets you focus human attention where it truly adds value (complex questions, nuanced discussions, etc.).

Small consultancies can also use AI to be proactive in client communications. Consider setting up automated status updates or check-ins. For example, if you're an IT consultant managing a client's project, an AI could be monitoring the system and can automatically alert the client "everything is running smoothly this week" or flag "we noticed a minor issue that is being resolved" – all without you drafting an email. Similarly, AI-driven CRM systems can analyze customer interactions across email, calls, and social media to let you know if a client might be at risk of dissatisfaction, so you can reach out before a small issue becomes a big problem. This predictive aspect of AI in client engagement helps a small firm *punch above its weight* in client care, catching things early as a larger firm's dedicated client success team might.

Tailoring and personalization. AI also empowers a high degree of personalization in your service delivery. For instance, you can use AI-driven proposal generators to tailor each client pitch or project proposal to their specific needs. Instead of using a one-size-fits-all deck, an AI tool can pull in relevant industry data, insert the client's name and context throughout, and adjust the tone and content based on their preferences. If you know a client values data, the AI will emphasize charts and analytics; if another values storytelling, it might start the proposal with a compelling narrative scenario. These generators leverage large language models to ensure the wording is polished and persuasive, and some even integrate with your CRM to include the client's unique context. According to a Motion study, businesses are turning to AI proposal generators because they save time and improve proposal quality through data-driven content – every proposal can be well-researched and customized without burning the midnight oil. By automating the heavy lifting of draft creation, you can produce comprehensive, personalized proposals in minutes instead of days, giving you an edge in persuasiveness and allowing you to respond to opportunities faster.

Personalization extends to day-to-day client interactions as well. AI tools can help you deliver concierge-level service by remembering client details and preferences. For example, an AI scheduling assistant might note that one client prefers morning meetings and automatically accommodate that. Or an AI email assistant can remind you, "It's been 3 months since the client's last strategy review – time for a personalized check-in," and even draft a message highlighting a few industry trends relevant to their business. This kind of tailored engagement makes the client feel valued and understood, *as if you have a whole team doing background research just for them.* In reality, it's your AI combing through data and prepping insights so you can have more informed conversations.

Data-informed insights for clients. One of the most exciting ways AI amplifies a consultant's value is by providing continuous, data-driven insights that you can pass on to clients. For instance, natural language processing tools can be set up to summarize your client's industry news daily. Each morning, you could receive an AI-curated brief: "Key news in client X's industry – new competitor entry, relevant regulatory change, trending consumer opinion on social media." With minimal effort, you stay on top of developments that impact your client. This means when you meet the client or have a weekly call, you're already informed and can proactively advise ("Have you considered how the new regulation Y might affect our strategy? I saw some analysis this week…"). Clients will notice that you always seem to have timely knowledge at your fingertips. Essentially, AI helps *turn information overload into actionable intelligence.* Small firms can leverage this to act like an "extended team" that is always watching out for the client's interests.

Another aspect is using AI analytics to deliver more tangible results. For example, AI-driven marketing tools could analyze a client's campaign data and suggest optimizations – perhaps identifying that certain customer segments respond better to a different message. You as the consultant receive these AI insights and can quickly adjust the strategy, delivering improved results in real time. In an accounting advisory context, an AI might rapidly crunch a client's financial data to produce forecasts and risk analyses that inform your advice. One report highlighted that AI can sift through large datasets to produce accurate forecasts and predictive insights, enabling small firms to offer highly personalized advice that strengthens client relationships and outcomes.

By leveraging historical data and AI predictions, a consultant can guide a client's decisions (like budget allocations or expansion plans) with evidence-backed confidence. This not only differentiates your service (you're providing analysis that used to require a whole analytics team) but also *builds trust*, as clients see the rationale behind your recommendations.

Meeting high client expectations. In the past, a small consultancy might have struggled to meet the responsiveness and depth that big firms offer. Now, AI is helping to erase that disadvantage. Clients today expect rapid turnarounds and comprehensive service without paying premium prices – essentially, *they want the cake and to eat it too.* AI enables you to deliver faster responses and thorough insights without burning out your team or breaking the bank. For instance, what happens when a client emails a question at 9 PM? With a tiny staff, that might wait until morning. But with AI, you could have a chatbot or an AI drafting an immediate acknowledgement with some initial info, or even working on the analysis overnight so that by morning you have a full answer ready. Similarly, when a client asks a complex question ("What are the latest consumer trends in our target market?"), an AI can swiftly gather data and provide a summary so you can respond knowledgeably in hours instead of weeks.

The end result is that a nimble, AI-augmented firm can feel to the client like a dedicated, around-the-clock partner. You're always available (through smart automation), always informed (through AI research), and always efficient (through streamlined processes). This elevates the client's experience – they get the attentiveness and expertise they crave. One could say that AI allows a small firm to offer *big-firm service quality with small-firm personalization.* You remain the expert and relationship builder, but you're amplified by AI in every interaction. Clients notice the difference: quicker answers, more frequent valuable touchpoints, and advice that's backed by data and seems one step ahead of the market.

Importantly, AI augments your expertise, it doesn't replace it. The human element – your creativity, empathy, and domain knowledge – remains at the core of professional services. AI just equips you with super-tools to execute and deliver that expertise more effectively. When you integrate AI into client engagement, you position your firm as innovative, responsive, and deeply attuned to client needs. Over time, this can translate to stronger client loyalty and word-of-mouth referrals, because working with you feels like getting the best of both worlds (personal attention *and* cutting-edge capabilities).

To put it in perspective, even traditionally cautious industries like law have found that AI helps small firms achieve a client service level competitive with larger practices. Solo and small law firms using AI report being able to turn work around faster, provide more strategic guidance, and be as responsive as big firms – effectively "competing like the big guys" thanks to AI-driven efficiencies. The lesson for all consulting and professional services is clear: embracing AI means you can deliver exceptional client value without needing the manpower and budgets of a Fortune 500 company.

Case Study – Transforming a Small Firm through AI

To illustrate all these points, let's look at a real-world inspired example of a boutique consulting agency that adopted AI solutions and saw dramatic improvements. We'll call this firm "Insight Advisors" – a small management consultancy with a team of five. Insight Advisors had a solid client roster but faced growing pains common to small firms. Their challenges included:

- Bottlenecks in research and analysis: With limited staff, in-depth research for client projects was slow. Complex data analysis (like reviewing client sales data or market research) would monopolize consultants' time, delaying reports and recommendations. They often felt they were scratching the surface of insights because they simply couldn't manually crunch more data in the time available.

- Administrative overload: Every team member wore multiple hats. Consultants spent part of their day on scheduling, note-taking, invoicing, and writing routine reports. These manual processes were inefficient – e.g. invoicing at month-end took two full days of work, and proposal writing for new clients was a dreaded, time-consuming task. There was no dedicated support staff, so high-value consulting time was lost to low-value admin tasks.

- Slow client response and limited value-add: If a client had an off-cycle request or an urgent question, Insight Advisors struggled to respond quickly while juggling other projects. They provided good advice, but it was mostly reactive. They knew that if they had more bandwidth for proactive analysis and communication, they could deliver more value and impress clients, but the day-to-day tasks left them in firefighting mode. In short, they risked seeming "small" to clients in terms of responsiveness and depth.

The firm's principal decided to bring in an AI consultant and invest in a suite of AI tools to tackle these pain points head-on. This transformation didn't happen overnight, but step by step, Insight Advisors integrated AI into their operations:

1. AI-powered research and analytics: They started by deploying an AI analytics platform (comparable to having a junior data analyst on call). This tool could securely ingest their clients' data – such as sales figures, customer surveys, web analytics – and instantly perform analysis that used to take weeks. In one case, a client had thousands of customer feedback entries from various channels. The AI platform analyzed all of it and identified clear patterns (top customer pain points and feature requests), which Insight Advisors could now present as data-backed insights in their strategy workshop. They also used AI to scan industry news and reports relevant to each client. Instead of one consultant spending days reading and compiling trends, an AI service would deliver a concise briefing each week. This move immediately boosted the firm's research capabilities – they began uncovering business insights that had been hard to see before, simply because they never had time to delve into such depth manually. Now, clients were getting more rigorous analysis and sooner.

2. Automating routine tasks: Next, Insight Advisors addressed the operational bottlenecks. They implemented an AI scheduling assistant on their website and email. Potential and existing clients could book meetings through a chatbot that synced with all consultants' calendars. The bot handled time zones, rescheduling, and meeting reminders automatically. No more back-and-forth emails – within a month, this saved countless hours and clients loved the instant booking confirmations. They also set up an AI-driven document management system: when a new client project kicked off, the AI would generate a draft project plan and checklist based on the scope (using past proposals and knowledge as a model), which consultants could then customize. For invoicing and data entry, they integrated an AI service that extracted data from timesheets and expense receipts and prepared draft invoices, cutting the billing process from two days to a few hours. A small law office might use a similar approach – for instance, Clio's AI features can automatically organize case files and schedule client meetings, tasks that used to consume hours of staff time. At Insight Advisors, once these administrative tasks were automated, the team suddenly had extra hours each week. One consultant remarked that it felt like they'd hired a part-time assistant, except this "assistant" worked tirelessly and virtually for free.

3. AI-enhanced client engagement: The firm also wanted to improve the client experience directly. They deployed a custom AI chatbot (trained on their company's knowledge base and

common consulting Q&As) on their website and as a contact point. This AI could handle basic client queries like, "What services do you offer? How do we start a project?" and even more specific questions, "Can you explain what this term in the report means?" Because it was fed with their past reports and context, it often could provide useful answers immediately, or at least acknowledge the query and promise a follow-up. Clients testing this out got immediate responses at any hour – making Insight Advisors look highly responsive and "always on." Internally, the team used an AI email assistant integrated with their CRM to ensure personalized follow-ups. After each client meeting, the AI would draft a follow-up email summarizing key points and next steps (pulled from the meeting transcript or notes) and schedule it to send within 24 hours. This meant every client consistently received a thoughtful recap without delay. These enhancements made clients feel more attended to and impressed by the firm's efficiency. In essence, AI helped Insight Advisors be available to clients 24/7 in some capacity and to respond with impressive speed on routine matters – something even larger firms sometimes struggle with.

4. Training and culture shift: Adopting AI tools required a culture shift at the firm. Initially, a couple of team members were skeptical – would the AI be accurate? Would it be hard to use? To address this, the firm invested in training sessions so everyone learned how to work alongside the new AI tools. They held workshops where employees practiced tasks with AI (like

reviewing the AI's draft of a report and refining it) to build confidence. They also encouraged an innovation mindset, reassuring staff that AI was there to assist, not replace them. Over a few months, the team grew comfortable and even enthusiastic as they saw the AI reducing drudgery in their jobs. One consultant joked that the AI tools were like the best intern they'd ever had – eager to do the boring stuff and *never complaining*. By fostering this collaborative culture, the firm ensured the technology was utilized fully and effectively.

The outcomes were impressive. Within the first year of this AI-driven transformation, Insight Advisors saw measurable gains that astonished them:

- Speed and productivity: Project turnaround times improved dramatically. Research that used to take two weeks was now done in two days, allowing the firm to deliver results to clients faster. Internally, they noticed that operational efficiency jumped – with AI handling repetitive work, consultants could dedicate ~30% more of their time to client-facing and strategic activities. In fact, a case study of a similar small business that embraced AI reported a significant uptick in productivity and sales, largely because AI-powered insights enabled more personalized and timely marketing efforts. Insight Advisors experienced the same; freeing up human bandwidth meant they could take on an extra few projects a quarter, effectively scaling up revenue without adding headcount.

- Cost savings and lower overhead: Automating tasks also translated to direct cost savings. The firm avoided the need to hire an additional administrative assistant or junior analyst, saving tens of thousands of dollars. Routine processes that once incurred errors (and thus extra time to fix) were now more error-proof thanks to AI's consistency. Overall, operational costs dropped – for example, they reduced the overtime hours they used to log during peak reporting periods, since AI took a chunk of that load. One real small business case recorded a *30% increase in sales and reduced operational costs after automating repetitive tasks*, which aligns with what Insight Advisors found. Essentially, AI allowed them to do more with the same budget, improving profit margins.

- Improved client satisfaction and retention: The feedback from clients was overwhelmingly positive. Clients noted the faster report delivery and the quick responses to inquiries. Several long-term clients expanded their contracts, impressed that this small firm was now providing service and insights on par with (or better than) larger consultancies they had worked with. The firm conducted a client satisfaction survey and saw scores climb notably compared to the previous year – clients specifically cited "responsiveness" and "data insights" as strengths. In quantitative terms, customer satisfaction scores increased and retention improved (no major clients left that year, whereas previously a couple might drift away annually). By delivering more value (through deeper analysis and proactive advice) and being there when needed (through AI-enhanced availability), Insight Advisors cemented loyalty among its client base.

- Revenue growth and new business: With operations running smoother, the firm had more capacity to focus on growth. They ramped up their marketing (using AI tools to assist in content creation and targeting the right prospects) and could handle a higher volume of leads thanks to the automated scheduling and proposal drafting. Over the year, they landed several new clients, including ones that normally might hire bigger firms. One new client mentioned they chose Insight Advisors because *"it felt like working with a cutting-edge team – they were small but had capabilities that others our size didn't."* The personalized, data-driven marketing campaigns – guided by AI analytics – led to a notable uptick in leads and conversions, directly boosting sales. By the year's end, the boutique firm's revenue had grown significantly, without a proportional increase in costs.

Insight Advisors' journey shows that even in a "people business" like consulting, leveraging AI can lead to improved service quality and business growth. What's key is how the AI was used: to augment the human team, not replace it. The consultants still did the critical thinking, relationship-building, and nuanced decision-making, but AI expanded what they could handle and the speed at which they could operate. The firm became more scalable – they could take on larger projects and more clients with confidence that their small team (plus AI) could deliver results comparable to a much larger organization.

This case study echoes a broader trend: small firms equipped with AI are now delivering work that rivals big firm outputs, *at a fraction of the cost and with greater agility*. It's no wonder industry experts are saying businesses should rethink paying hefty fees to big consultancies "when smaller entities, equipped with AI, can deliver equal or superior value at a fraction of the cost." The transformation of Insight Advisors underscores that AI implementation isn't just about tech – it's about empowering talented people in a small business to amplify their impact. By embracing AI, the firm overcame its bottlenecks and turned them into strengths: research became a selling point, not a slow grind; operations became lean, not a hassle; client service became a differentiator, not a pain point.

As we conclude this chapter, the story of Insight Advisors (and many real firms like it) drives home an inspiring message: size no longer has to dictate your capability. A two-person consultancy or a ten-lawyer firm can genuinely compete with organizations ten times their size by smartly deploying AI. The playing field in professional services is being leveled by technology. For those willing to innovate, this is a tremendous opportunity. Small firms can be *both* highly personalized and tech-augmented powerhouses. By automating, scaling, and augmenting your work with free or low-cost AI tools, you truly gain the *Small Business AI Advantage* – delivering big value, punching above your weight, and carving out a competitive edge in the marketplace of expertise. The experience of firms like Insight Advisors shows that leveraging AI is not just about efficiency; it's about amplifying your expertise to achieve outcomes that once seemed out of reach for a small business. That is the new advantage – and it's one any small consulting or professional service firm can seize.

Chapter 5

AI in Digital Marketing – Doing More With Less

Content Creation and Creative Design at Scale

Small businesses often struggle to produce a steady stream of high-quality marketing content due to limited staff and time. Crafting blog posts, social media updates, and graphics is labor-intensive, especially for a small agency or a solo business owner without a dedicated creative team. Fortunately, modern AI tools are becoming invaluable creative assistants that help generate and inspire content on demand. These tools can write text for various marketing needs – from full blog articles to catchy social media captions – and even assist in basic graphic design. The result is that a small business can maintain a strong marketing presence without an army of copywriters and designers.

One clear example is the experience of Fringe, a boutique brand design company whose owner was initially skeptical about AI copywriting. After his first use of an AI writing tool (Copy.ai) during a bout of writer's block, he realized the algorithm was far more useful than expected: the AI quickly produced on-brand text for everything from Instagram captions to product descriptions, freeing his team from their writer's block. In fact, the Fringe team found they could generate "rows of copy" for both client projects and their own brand in a fraction of the time, solving writing issues that had lingered for months or years. The AI platform not only saved them hours of writing but also sparked new ideas, providing content inspiration based on real-time data from the web. This allowed the small team to focus more on strategy and creative refinement, rather than getting bogged down in drafting copy from scratch.

Beyond text generation, AI is also making visual content creation more accessible on a tight budget. In the past, designing graphics or editing videos might require professional software skills or outsourcing to specialists. Today, however, a variety of AI image and video generation tools have emerged that can create visuals with minimal effort or cost. For instance, AI image generators like DALL-E 2 can produce custom images and artwork from a simple text description – ideal for a small business that needs original illustrations or product mockups for social media and web content without hiring a graphic designer. On the video side, tools such as Pictory act as an AI video creator for small businesses, making it easy to turn a script or even an existing blog post into a short, sharable video complete with stock footage or AI-generated visuals. Essentially, these platforms handle the heavy lifting of design: a business owner can input their content or ideas, and the AI generates polished visual materials ready for posting. The key takeaway is that AI can serve as a creative partner, amplifying the output of a tiny marketing team. This enables a volume and consistency of content that would have been out of reach just a few years ago. With AI generating first drafts and design mockups, small businesses can do more creative production with less manual labor, leveling the playing field with larger competitors.

Precision Targeting and Analytics (Marketing to the Right Audience)

When resources are scarce, every marketing dollar must count. Unlike big corporations, small businesses can't afford to aim ads and campaigns at the wrong audience and hope something sticks. This is where AI-driven marketing analytics give smaller players a powerful advantage – the ability to pinpoint the right customers and make data-driven decisions so that promotional budgets are spent wisely. Even a modest marketing team can now leverage AI tools to analyze customer data, discover patterns, and target campaigns with laser precision.

One of AI's strengths is finding meaningful patterns in vast customer data that a human might miss. AI algorithms excel at grouping consumers into segments based on their behaviors and preferences, essentially creating refined "audience clusters" that share common traits. By examining factors like purchase history, browsing activity, and demographics, AI can automatically segment a customer base in a very granular way. These insights allow a business to tailor messages and offers to each group, personalizing marketing content for better resonance. Instead of sending the same generic promotion to everyone, a small business could have one message for frequent buyers, another for budget-conscious shoppers, and yet another for those who only browse certain product categories – all determined with AI's help. Research shows that this kind of AI-driven audience segmentation leads to higher engagement and conversion rates because each customer feels the marketing speaks directly to their needs.

AI-based analytics platforms are making such precision targeting accessible through user-friendly tools. They can automatically identify distinct customer segments and even suggest what products or services each segment is most likely to be interested in. For example, an AI-driven marketing application might analyze an e-commerce site's data and reveal that a significant cluster of customers – say, young parents buying eco-friendly products – was previously overlooked in advertising. Equipped with this insight, the business can create a tailored campaign for that segment (perhaps a special eco-friendly family product bundle or targeted social media ads on parenting pages). In fact, deep learning algorithms have been used to identify untapped opportunities in customer data – uncovering potential buyer groups and niche markets that a small business didn't even realize existed. By discovering these hidden segments, small firms can expand their customer base strategically, guided by data rather than hunches.

Another area where AI shines is predictive analytics, which helps small businesses not just look at historical data but also forecast future trends. Predictive marketing tools can analyze past customer behavior and seasonal patterns to answer questions like: *When is the best time to run a holiday promotion? Which product categories are likely to surge next month?* By forecasting sales trends or engagement spikes, AI helps in planning campaigns at optimal times and stocking the right inventory to meet anticipated demand. Moreover, AI can continuously monitor campaign performance in real time and adjust targeting parameters on the fly. If certain ads are performing poorly with one demographic but exceptionally well with another, the AI can reallocate budget or suggest a change in strategy almost instantly. This kind of responsive optimization, which might take a human analyst days or weeks to implement, can happen in hours with AI-driven tools. The result is maximum ROI: every dollar is directed where it's most likely to generate returns. Even small marketing teams are using affordable AI platforms that unify data from web analytics, social media, and CRM systems, giving them a level of insight once reserved for enterprises with dedicated data science teams. By trusting these data-driven insights, small businesses can confidently decide *who* to target, *when* to run campaigns, and *how* to personalize their messaging – ensuring that their limited marketing budget punches above its weight.

As a result, small businesses can engage in smart marketing: reaching the right people with the right message, at the right time, and with the right offer. It's marketing to the *right* audience, not just the largest audience, and it's fueled by evidence rather than guesswork. Ultimately, AI-enabled targeting means small enterprises no longer have to "spray and pray" with their marketing – they can compete with Fortune 500s by being strategic and efficient, doing more with less waste.

Social Media Automation and Customer Engagement

Managing an active social media presence can feel like a second full-time job for many small business owners. Keeping up with posting schedules, responding to comments, and engaging followers across multiple platforms (Facebook, Instagram, Twitter, LinkedIn, etc.) is a major time sink. AI comes to the rescue here as a sort of virtual social media manager, automating routine tasks and enhancing how businesses interact with their online audience. The goal is to maintain a lively and responsive social media profile without requiring the owner or a small team to be glued to their screens 24/7.

One way AI helps is through smart scheduling and content planning. Instead of manually figuring out when and what to post, small businesses can use AI-powered social media management tools that automatically schedule posts at optimal times and even suggest content ideas. These tools analyze when your followers are most active and what topics are trending, then recommend the best times and themes for new posts to maximize engagement. For instance, an AI platform might identify that your Instagram audience engages most on weekday evenings, and queue up your posts for those slots. Modern social media suites like Smartly.io and Ocoya provide one-stop solutions for these needs: they let users create or curate content, auto-generate captions and hashtags, schedule posts across multiple channels, and then analyze the results – all in one dashboard. By consolidating these tasks, an AI-driven platform ensures consistency (no more forgetting to post during a busy week) and strategic timing (each post goes out when it's likely to have the biggest impact).

AI can also assist in content curation by monitoring social trends. Small teams no longer need to spend hours researching what's popular or viral; AI systems can scan social media in real time and pinpoint which topics, memes, or hashtags are gaining traction. Armed with this insight, a business can quickly create a post that rides a trending wave, joining the conversation while it's still hot. For example, an AI analysis might reveal that a particular hashtag or topic relevant to your industry is surging in popularity this week – something a human might notice too late. With AI, you could get an alert and promptly publish content that capitalizes on that trend, allowing your brand to insert itself into the discussion at just the right moment. In this way, a small business can stay culturally relevant and engaging without needing a dedicated team of trend-watchers. Additionally, AI writing assistants can draft social media captions or generate variations of posts tailored to each platform, ensuring the tone and format are optimized for different channels (for example, concise text for Twitter, visual emphasis for Instagram, professional wording for LinkedIn).

Beyond scheduling and content creation, AI plays an important role in direct customer engagement on social platforms. One growing practice is using AI-driven chatbots to interact with customers via social media messaging (like Facebook Messenger) or on the business's own website through live chat. These AI chatbots can handle common inquiries and tasks automatically, providing instant responses at any hour. For a small business, having a chatbot is like having a customer service rep who works 24/7 without breaks. They greet users who visit your Facebook page or website, answer frequently asked questions (store hours, product availability, return policies, etc.), and guide customers toward making a purchase by suggesting products or helping with checkout issues. Importantly, these bots use natural language processing to understand questions and respond in a conversational way, so customers feel heard and helped. For example, a visitor to a boutique's online store might ask, "Do you have this item in size M?" – an AI agent can immediately check the inventory database and respond, or offer to notify the user when the item is back in stock. This kind of responsiveness was previously only possible if someone was always available to monitor chats.

The advantage of AI-driven chatbots for a small business cannot be overstated. They dramatically improve responsiveness – customers get answers in seconds rather than waiting hours for an email reply. They also ensure consistency in customer service by always providing polite, accurate information drawn from a knowledge base. And they lighten the workload on human staff, who can focus on complex inquiries while routine ones (like "Where's my order?" or "What are your prices?") are handled automatically. According to one account, AI-based chatbots offer an inexpensive way for small businesses to handle customer questions *around the clock* without needing a large support team – and they use NLP to respond within seconds, answer common queries, track orders, process returns, and even recommend products, all without human intervention. By taking over these initial interactions, AI agents capture leads and assist customers even when the human team is off the clock. In essence, a small business with an AI chatbot can provide *big-business* customer service – prompt, personalized, and always available – projecting a level of professionalism and attentiveness that helps build customer trust.

Another benefit of AI in social media management is the simplification of multi-channel campaigns. The same AI platform can manage your Facebook, Instagram, Twitter, and other profiles in an integrated way – scheduling coordinated posts and tailoring content to each platform's format automatically. It then aggregates the performance data across channels to show what's working best. By analyzing this data, the AI learns which content types and posting strategies yield the highest engagement for your audience, and it refines its recommendations over time. This means your multi-channel social strategy keeps improving continuously, without the need for constant manual adjustment.

By automating social media scheduling and initial customer interactions, small businesses free up valuable time and ensure no inquiry falls through the cracks. Imagine a customer leaves a comment on your product post asking about compatibility – an AI system could auto-reply with a helpful answer or at least acknowledge the question and promise a follow-up. Meanwhile, the business owner can focus on higher-level tasks like product development or closing sales, confident that the online audience is being engaged. In sum, AI allows a tiny team to handle social media as if they had a full-fledged department. The business remains active and responsive on social networks at all times, helping them punch above their weight in digital presence and customer service. A consistent, quick social media interaction can make customers feel valued and heard, which in turn strengthens brand loyalty even for a very small company.

Case Study – AI-Powered Marketing Campaign Success

For a tangible example of AI in small business marketing, consider how a boutique agency used AI to achieve outsized results in email and advertising campaigns. Agency Pure, a full-service advertising agency, decided to supercharge its email marketing by integrating an AI-driven email newsletter platform called *rasa.io*. Like many small agencies, Agency Pure's team was stretched thin and found it difficult to deliver deeply personalized content to each of their newsletter subscribers. They were sending a generic newsletter to all clients and prospects, and leadership was skeptical that investing a lot of time into it would pay off. In an era of overflowing inboxes, they feared detailed segmentation or one-to-one customization might come off as insincere to clients – and frankly, they didn't have the time to manually craft different content for every reader.

Rasa.io changed the game for them. The AI analyzed each subscriber's interests and engagement history (e.g. which links a person clicked or what topics they read most) and automatically customized the newsletter content for each individual. In other words, Subscriber A might receive an email full of social media marketing tips, while Subscriber B's copy features more branding and design articles – all personalized by the algorithm. Agency Pure understood the value of such personalization but had never been able to do it manually (it would be nearly impossible without AI). With the AI handling this level of detail, the process happened effortlessly in the background. Almost immediately after launching their AI-personalized newsletter, Agency Pure saw email open rates and click-through rates climb significantly – and they continued to rise. This was a clear sign that readers were more engaged, as the content they received was more relevant to their interests. The small agency achieved what felt like a one-to-one conversation with each subscriber, courtesy of AI. This story illustrates how AI can unlock capabilities that small marketing teams simply couldn't manage before. By automating the data-crunching and personalization, the human marketers at Agency Pure were free to focus on strategy and creative work, while the AI handled the repetitive task of tailoring content to individual tastes.

Another success story in AI-powered marketing comes from the world of online advertising. A mid-sized marketing agency (not a Fortune 500, just a local firm) wanted to improve the performance of the Facebook and Instagram ads it ran for clients. They ran an experiment using an AI tool called Pattern89 to optimize one ad campaign, while running a similar ad campaign without AI assistance as a control. Over two weeks, the AI-managed campaign continuously analyzed engagement data and adjusted the ads (tweaking imagery, budget, targeting, etc.) on the fly. The final outcome proved the power of AI: the Pattern89-optimized campaign achieved an 81% lower cost per result and 439% higher conversion rate on the same ad spend as the human-managed campaign, even earning 11% more impressions. In short, the AI-driven ads were vastly more efficient and effective. This experiment showed that even a smaller agency could leverage AI to drastically outperform a traditional approach – a clear example of a transformative win rather than just a minor improvement.

In conclusion, the theme "Doing More With Less" truly resonates through each of this chapter's examples. Whether it's content creation, audience targeting, social engagement, or running ad campaigns, AI enables small organizations to operate at a scale and sophistication previously reserved for those with far greater resources. A tiny team can tap into AI tools – many of them free or low-cost – to automate tedious tasks, uncover hidden opportunities, and execute marketing initiatives with precision. The Small Business AI Advantage is real: a two-person startup can gain the analytic insights of a big data department, a one-person marketing shop can produce content with the consistency of a full agency, and a busy owner can deliver 24/7 customer service that rivals larger firms. In short, the playing field between the local business and the corporate giant becomes more level when AI is involved. And the payoff isn't just time saved (though that's huge) – it's results that weren't possible before. Higher engagement, better conversion rates, stronger customer loyalty – these are the kinds of transformative outcomes even the smallest business can achieve by intelligently deploying AI in digital marketing. In this way, AI truly lets small businesses do more with less, turning limited resources into a competitive advantage.

Chapter 6

AI in Manufacturing and Operations – Smart, Lean, and Agile

Automation and Robotics for Small-Scale Production

Advanced manufacturing tech isn't just for mega-factories anymore – even modest workshops and 50-person plants can now leverage AI-driven automation on their shop floors. In fact, small manufacturers today are gaining the scale, speed, and quality advantages to compete with larger firms through the use of robotics. The bottom line, as one industry expert put it, is that automation and robotics allow small manufacturers to compete and win more deals as effectively as their larger competitors. This democratization of robotics means that a family-owned factory can achieve efficiency gains once reserved for companies ten times its size.

Figure above: A collaborative robotic arm performing a fabric-cutting operation in a small garment workshop, demonstrating how AI-driven robotics can handle intricate tasks even in smaller production settings.

AI-powered machines – from simple robotic arms to sophisticated collaborative robots (cobots) – are now available as relatively affordable, modular systems. Robotics providers have introduced entry-level models and even "robotics-as-a-service" offerings to lower the barrier for small businesses. In fact, the *average price of an industrial robot has halved over the past decade*, dropping from about $47,000 in 2011 to $23,000 in 2022, and is projected to fall by another 50–60% by 2025. This plunge in cost, combined with easier programming and safer designs, has opened the door for small shops to deploy robots on a budget. It's no surprise that smaller manufacturers are now the fastest-growing segment of industrial robotics adoption, especially via flexible cobots that can work side-by-side with humans.

These robots can take over repetitive, tedious, or dangerous tasks on the production line, boosting productivity and reducing human error. For example, even a tiny machine shop can install a robotic arm to handle welding, sorting, or packaging tasks with precision and consistency. The AI-guided robot follows instructions to perform each operation the same way every time, which minimizes errors and frees human workers from risky or monotonous duties. Collaborative robots are designed to be safe around people, so they can literally work shoulder-to-shoulder with your team – think of a cobot gently assisting an employee by lifting heavy parts or applying glue in exact amounts. This human-robot teamwork allows small operations to run faster and more efficiently without overwhelming their staff.

One real-world example illustrates the impact well. A small plastics manufacturer in the Pacific Northwest struggled to hire enough workers for a big order of medical device kits. Instead of turning down the business, they piloted a pair of robotic stackers and sorters. The result: by running the robots across three shifts, this little shop was able to deliver 150,000 kits per week for their client – a throughput that would have been impossible otherwise. The robots handled the repetitive picking and packing, while the few human operators focused on quality and supervision. This story shows how a small factory can punch above its weight with automation.

It's also important to note that labor shortages are a driving force pushing small companies toward automation. Manufacturers everywhere face *"huge problems recruiting and retaining employees,"* as Harvard Business Review observed, with over 2 million U.S. manufacturing jobs projected to go unfilled by the end of the decade. Small businesses feel this pinch acutely. Deploying robots can alleviate the pressure – the cobot doesn't call in sick or quit, and can fill in gaps on the assembly line. Far from replacing humans entirely, these AI-driven machines complement your workforce by taking on the dull and dangerous tasks, while your human employees can focus on higher-value work. The net effect is a smarter, leaner, and more agile production floor where a nimble small company can achieve big-league productivity.

Predictive Maintenance and Quality Control

Downtime and defects are the twin enemies of any manufacturer. For small firms with tight margins, an unexpected machine breakdown or a batch of flawed products can be especially devastating. Here's where AI offers a game-changing solution: predictive maintenance systems to prevent breakdowns and automated quality control to prevent defects before they reach customers.

Predictive maintenance uses AI and sensors to continuously monitor equipment health in real time, alerting business owners to signs of wear or impending failure before a machine actually breaks. Traditional maintenance either follows a fixed schedule (which can take machines offline unnecessarily) or reacts to failures (which causes costly downtime). AI enables a smarter approach: tiny sensors on your machines collect data on vibrations, temperature, noise, power draw and more, and machine-learning models sift through this data in real time. The AI learns what "normal" looks like for each piece of equipment and can flag subtle deviations minutes or even days before a breakdown would occur. For instance, if a motor's vibration pattern or heat output starts to drift outside the normal range, the system might predict a bearing failure brewing. It will instantly send an alert with an analysis – perhaps even estimating the remaining useful life of the part – so you can schedule maintenance at the next convenient downtime. Maintenance teams can then replace that bearing *before* it fails catastrophically, ideally timing the fix for a lunch break or off-shift to avoid any impact on production.

The benefits of this AI-driven approach are huge. Manufacturers that have adopted predictive analytics have seen significantly less unplanned downtime – some report 50% fewer surprise equipment failures after implementing these systems. For a small business, that could mean the difference between meeting your delivery deadlines or scrambling to explain to customers why their order is late. By intervening early, you also avoid secondary damage (preventing a small fault from cascading into a major machine wreck) and extend the lifespan of your equipment. One industry analysis noted that moving from reactive fixes to AI-based preventive upkeep not only cuts downtime, it also trims maintenance costs by 20% or more and adds years to the life of machines. And as a bonus, a well-maintained line is safer for workers – no more sudden mechanical failures creating hazards. In short, AI keeps your machines happy and humming, so your operation stays lean and productive.

On the quality control side, AI is helping even the smallest manufacturers achieve near-zero defect rates. Traditionally, quality inspection in a small plant meant a few human inspectors eyeballing products on the line or testing random samples. Humans, however, get tired and can miss subtle flaws – especially when throughput is high. AI changes the game with computer vision and pattern recognition. AI-powered quality control systems use cameras and image analysis algorithms to automatically inspect products at high speed, in real time. These systems can detect defects that might be missed by human inspection, ensuring that only high-quality goods reach consumers. For example, an AI vision system can spot a tiny stitching error on a garment or a minute hairline crack in a machined part far better than a person could. It "sees" every item on the line and compares it against the ideal pattern. If anything falls outside of acceptable tolerance – a wrong color shade, a misaligned label, a surface flaw – the AI flags it and the item can be removed or reworked immediately.

The payoff is tremendous for a small manufacturer: you catch issues early, *before* faulty products go out the door. That means far fewer customer returns and warranty claims, less waste and rework, and a consistently reliable product quality that becomes a competitive advantage. One guide notes that by identifying even minor flaws in real time, AI visual inspection ensures consistent quality and lets small factories maintain high standards without slowing down production. In practical terms, that consistency translates into dollars saved. Fewer defects and do-overs mean you're not scrapping materials or paying labor a second time to fix mistakes – an AI quality system directly reduces waste and production costs. Just as importantly, your reputation with customers improves when they can trust that every delivery will meet specs. Using cutting-edge tech to achieve near-perfect quality gives even a small shop an aura of reliability that can enhance its brand reputation.

Crucially, these AI quality and maintenance solutions have become accessible to smaller manufacturers. Many are available via affordable subscription models or as add-ons to existing machinery. You don't need to rip out all your old equipment – you can retrofit sensors onto legacy machines and connect them to cloud-based AI platforms that analyze the data. Likewise, AI vision systems can often be installed above a production line or inside a test station and integrated with your current workflow. There are even companies offering "inspection-as-a-service" where you pay a monthly fee per camera or per number of parts inspected, which lowers the upfront cost. In other words, a small firm can implement these advanced capabilities without massive capital expenditure. The result is a more reliable, lean operation with fewer surprises. You spend less time putting out fires and more time consistently delivering good products. In the end, fewer faulty products (hence less waste and rework) and more uptime give small manufacturers a competitive edge through operational consistency.

Optimizing Production Planning and Supply Chain

Efficiency in operations is absolutely crucial for small businesses – margins are thin, and they can't afford excess inventory sitting idle or orders delayed by supply hiccups. AI has emerged as a powerful ally in production planning and supply chain management, helping even modest-sized manufacturers run as lean and agile as the best of the Fortune 500. By crunching vast amounts of data on sales, inventory, and supply trends, AI systems can optimize what to produce, when to produce it, and how to get it to the customer in the most efficient way.

On the production planning side, AI-driven software can analyze historical demand patterns, current orders, and even external factors (like seasonal trends or market indicators) to create an optimal manufacturing schedule. Instead of relying on gut feeling or static spreadsheets, a small manufacturer can use AI to decide what to produce, in what quantity, and at what time. For example, an AI scheduling tool might examine your last few years of sales data and detect that demand for a certain product spikes every February. It will then suggest ramping up production of that item in January so you're ready – but not too much, to avoid overproduction. If an unexpected large order comes in, the AI can dynamically adjust the schedule: it might rearrange other jobs, allocate extra machine time, or authorize overtime for that week, ensuring the big order is met *without* throwing the entire production line into chaos. Essentially, the AI acts like a smart operations manager 24/7, constantly tweaking the plan as conditions change. This means maximizing use of resources while still meeting customer demand just in time – no more piles of unsold stock, and no more missed delivery dates because of poor planning.

AI's impact on the supply chain is just as impressive. Small manufacturers often juggle dozens of materials and parts, and keeping the right amount in stock is a perpetual challenge – too much inventory ties up cash and storage space, while too little means you risk running out and halting production. AI-powered inventory management systems can solve this juggling act by tracking and forecasting inventory needs with precision. These systems connect to your inventory database, supplier lead times, and even market prices, and they use machine learning to forecast when you'll need to reorder each item. For instance, the AI might learn that a particular type of fabric or metal component tends to be delivered 10 days after ordering and that you use it at a rate of 100 units a week. If your on-hand quantity is about to drop below the safety level, the AI can automatically trigger a reorder *just in time* so that new stock arrives right as you need it. It can even optimize order quantities to take advantage of bulk pricing without overstocking. The goal is to avoid both shortages and overstock, freeing up cash while raising order fulfillment rates (having what the customer needs when they need it). In practice, companies using AI for demand forecasting and inventory have managed to keep their service levels high (few if any stockouts) while carrying significantly leaner inventory. In fact, small manufacturers who embrace these tools have cut inventory holding costs by an estimated 20–50% – money that goes straight back into the business.

AI can also help manage suppliers and logistics in smarter ways. An AI supply chain platform might monitor news feeds, weather reports, and transit data to predict potential disruptions – for example, warning you days in advance if a major storm could delay a shipment of raw materials at a port. The system could then suggest alternate suppliers or reroute shipments proactively. Some tools will automatically pick optimal shipping routes for your deliveries by analyzing real-time traffic and weather, ensuring the fastest or most cost-efficient path. Others might use natural language processing to read supplier emails or performance reports and alert you to any red flags (like a supplier consistently delivering late or having quality issues). The upshot is a supply chain that's not run on guesswork or frantic "firefighting," but rather on data-driven foresight. As GENEDGE, a manufacturing advisory organization, describes it, AI turns reactive supply chains into proactive ones, replacing guesswork with agility and helping even small firms protect their profit during chaos.

Let's consider a scenario to illustrate the impact. Imagine a 50-person company that makes custom furniture. In the past, they might have over-ordered lumber and hardware "just in case," tying up a lot of cash in inventory, yet still occasionally run short of a particular wood type and delay an order. After implementing an AI-driven planning and inventory system, things changed dramatically. The AI analyzed their historical sales and lead times and now forecasts exactly how much oak, maple, screws, and varnish they'll need each week. It automatically places orders with suppliers so that materials arrive exactly when production requires them. The result: the factory always has the right materials when needed, but no huge surplus. The company's carrying costs for inventory dropped substantially – in line with industry stats showing a 20–50% reduction in inventory holding cost after adopting AI optimization. At the same time, stockouts disappeared; they haven't had to tell a customer "we're waiting on material" in ages. If a sudden spike in orders comes in, the AI system immediately flags the need for extra materials and expedites shipping, while simultaneously adjusting the production schedule to ensure all orders are fulfilled. By streamlining its supply chain with AI, this small manufacturer prevented costly delays and excesses, essentially running a *lean, just-in-time operation* that would make a Fortune 500 firm proud.

Beyond day-to-day logistics, the data and insights from these AI tools also inform strategic decisions. Owners and managers get dashboards forecasting months ahead – showing, for example, that a certain product's demand is likely to grow 15% next quarter, or that a certain raw material might face a shortage in the market. Armed with this intelligence, a small manufacturer can plan proactively (perhaps securing an alternate supplier or scaling up marketing for a high-demand item) and thus seize opportunities or mitigate risks faster than competitors. In essence, AI gives the little guys a sophisticated planning brain that was once the exclusive luxury of big corporations. By leveraging historical and real-time data in tandem, these systems help predict future trends and guide strategic choices that give a small manufacturer a competitive edge.

Case Study – Small Manufacturer Goes High-Tech

To see all these concepts in action, let's profile a small manufacturer that embraced AI to transform its operations. Consider a *family-owned garment factory* with around 40 employees, making apparel for boutique brands. They were operating on thin margins (as is common in the clothing industry) and faced very high quality expectations from their clients. Even a few defects slipping through or any machine downtime could eat into their profits or jeopardize their customer relationships. Determined to rise above these challenges, the factory's owners decided to invest in AI solutions in two critical areas: quality control and machine maintenance.

Quality Control Upgrade: The factory integrated an AI-powered visual inspection system into its production line to check garments and fabrics in real time. They set up high-resolution cameras at key points – one scanning incoming fabrics for flaws, and another checking each finished garment for defects as it came off the sewing line. These cameras feed images to a computer-vision AI trained on what defects look like: a missing stitch, a misaligned seam, a tiny stain or hole, etc. Now, every single item is scrutinized by the unblinking eye of AI. The moment the system detects a flaw – say a barely noticeable stitching irregularity – it flags the item for removal or repair. The impact was immediate and striking. Errors that previously slipped through human inspection were suddenly caught by the AI. The factory went from relying on a couple of tired eyeballs to having a tireless automated inspector on duty 24/7. Over the first few months, the AI system consistently identified defects that had been causing customer returns in the past, and the team was able to correct them on the spot. As a result, the rate of defective products reaching customers plummeted. The company's return rates dropped dramatically – essentially, only good product was getting out the door.

One internal report noted that automated inspections reduced product defects by about 35%, which in turn cut rework and waste and enhanced the factory's reputation for quality. Indeed, the small factory's clients noticed the change: complaints and returned merchandise virtually disappeared, and positive feedback about the "consistent high quality" of the garments increased. This boost in quality has become a selling point for the business, helping it retain and attract customers who might otherwise go to larger, more established competitors. In short, by implementing AI vision technology, our small garment factory was able to achieve a level of quality control on par with (or even better than) much bigger operations. As one apparel tech team observed, *AI visual inspection catches even minor flaws and ensures consistent quality, enabling small factories to uphold high standards* – a truth this factory can firmly attest to now.

Predictive Maintenance Initiative: The second prong of the factory's AI strategy tackled machine downtime. The shop was filled with sewing machines and cutting equipment that were the lifeblood of the operation. Previously, if one of these machines broke down – a sewing machine motor burning out or a computerized cutter going offline – it could halt a whole production line until a technician fixed it. To prevent such incidents, the factory deployed a predictive maintenance system across their critical equipment. They equipped the sewing and cutting machines with IoT sensors that continuously monitored things like motor vibrations, temperature of the motors/needles, and operating speed. All this data streamed into an AI platform that learned the normal operating profile of each machine. Before long, the AI could pick up on the early-warning signs of mechanical issues. For instance, it might detect that one sewing machine's motor was running a little hot and vibrating more than usual – often a precursor to a part wearing out. The system would then alert the maintenance team with a notification like: "Machine 7 may need a new bearing in the next 10 hours of operation." Armed with this information, the team could fix or tune up Machine 7 during a scheduled break that very day, rather than waiting for it to fail mid-production. This approach minimized unplanned downtime to near zero. Over the course of the first year, the factory saw hardly any surprise breakdowns; the AI warnings allowed them to intervene in a controlled, planned way every time. The maintenance manager noted that this proactive upkeep reduced repair costs by about 20% – because they were fixing issues when they were minor and avoiding the expensive damage that occurs in a major breakdown. And of course, keeping the lines running smoothly meant orders kept flowing out on time. The factory's production efficiency ticked upward, contributing to better overall profitability.

Results and Reflections: By embracing AI in these targeted ways – quality control and maintenance – this small garment manufacturer achieved what could be called a "smart factory" makeover, but on a small-business budget. The efficiency gains were tangible: with fewer defects and less downtime, they were able to produce more sellable garments per week with the same workforce. Their scrap and rework costs went down, maintenance overtime went down, and customer satisfaction went up. In fact, after these implementations, the owners reported that customer returns virtually disappeared and on-time deliveries hit new highs, since there were no quality hold-ups or machine failures causing delays. The consistency in output also gave them the confidence to take on some larger orders they would have previously dreaded – they knew their process could handle it without cracking. Perhaps most importantly, the intangible benefits in reputation and employee morale have been significant. The company became known for its reliability and top-notch quality, helping it stand out in the market. Employees, initially nervous about "robots" and AI, found that these tools actually made their jobs easier and safer – they no longer had to strain to inspect hundreds of garments a day or rush to troubleshoot sudden machine crashes. Instead, they work alongside the AI, focusing on tasks that truly require human creativity and judgment, like solving process issues and improving designs.

This case underscores a powerful point: even a family-owned factory can achieve smart, lean, and agile operations by strategically implementing AI. You don't need to be a tech giant or invest millions to see results. By identifying key pain points (in this case, quality and downtime) and applying affordable AI tools, a small manufacturer can dramatically enhance its performance. As we've seen, the factory achieved efficiency and consistency improvements once thought to be the exclusive domain of much larger "Industry 4.0" players. Their story is a blueprint for other small businesses: pick your spots where AI can have the biggest impact, start small with pilot projects, and then scale up once you see the benefits. The *Small Business AI Advantage* is real – with the right approach, a nimble 50-person operation can leverage AI to automate, scale, and compete head-to-head with Fortune 500 manufacturers. This little garment factory did it, and so can others, ushering in a new era where size and resource limits are no longer a barrier to world-class manufacturing operations.

Chapter 7
Ethics, Data Privacy, and Regulatory Compliance – Safeguarding Your AI Strategy

Ethical AI Use and Bias Mitigation

With great power comes great responsibility. This famous adage (often attributed to Spider-Man's Uncle Ben) perfectly captures the challenge small businesses face with AI. AI can be a powerful engine for growth, but it must be used responsibly. In this section, we tackle the ethical considerations you need to keep in mind when deploying AI in your business. The core idea is simple: ensure your AI tools help your customers and your reputation, not hurt them. That means being alert to issues like bias and unfairness in AI decisions, and taking proactive steps to mitigate them.

Consider the risk of bias in AI systems. AI makes decisions based on data – and if that data reflects historical prejudices or imbalances, the AI can inadvertently perpetuate them. A now-famous example involved Amazon's experimental hiring AI. The tool was trained on ten years of past resumes, most of which came from men (since the tech industry was male-dominated). The result? The AI "taught itself" that male candidates were preferable. It even penalized resumes that included the word "women's," as in "women's chess club," effectively downranking female applicants. Amazon's engineers discovered this issue and ultimately scrapped the tool, but the lesson was loud and clear: AI can reflect our biases if we're not careful. Similarly, in the financial world, the Apple Card made headlines when customers noticed something troubling – some women were getting far lower credit limits than their husbands, even with similar finances. Tech entrepreneur David Heinemeier Hansson tweeted that he got 20 times the credit limit his wife did, and even Apple's co-founder Steve Wozniak reported a 10× credit limit difference in favor of him over his wife. Goldman Sachs, the bank behind Apple Card, denied deliberate discrimination, but regulators launched an inquiry. The likely culprit was an algorithm making credit decisions that, unintentionally, ended up skewed. These real cases show that bias in AI isn't a theoretical worry – it can and does happen, even to big companies.

For a small business, the stakes are just as real (even if on a smaller scale). Imagine a small marketing firm using an AI tool to target ads or personalize offers. If that AI's training data has biases, it might start showing certain job ads only to men or offering discounts only in affluent ZIP codes. This could *exclude* or *unfairly target* groups of customers, undermining your values and exposing you to reputational damage or even legal risks. The key is not to throw your hands up in fear, but to deploy AI thoughtfully. Best practices for responsible AI use include keeping humans in the loop and establishing clear ethical guidelines from the get-go. In practice, "keeping humans in the loop" means that you or your team should oversee important AI-driven decisions, especially early on. Don't just set an AI on autopilot for critical tasks like hiring, lending, or content moderation without any oversight. Have a human review what the AI is recommending – does it make sense, is it fair, could it be missing something? By having that human checkpoint, you can catch odd or biased outputs and correct course. Think of AI as your super-smart intern: it can work through a stack of resumes or analyze customer data blazingly fast, but you (the experienced manager) still need to double-check its work and provide direction.

It also helps to implement what some call "AI ethics by design." This means baking your ethical principles into the AI's workflow and your company policies from day one. For example, if your company values diversity and fairness, make that a criterion when choosing or training an AI system. Use diverse training data where possible, and test your AI's outputs for bias periodically. Set ground rules like, "Our AI screening tool will never automatically reject a candidate – it will flag top candidates, but a human will always review and make the final call." By designing these guardrails, even a non-technical business owner can ensure their AI tools are *augmenting* human decision-making rather than blindly automating it. In fact, regulators and experts often recommend this "human in the loop" approach as a safety net for AI. For instance, some state bar associations in the legal field now explicitly require that if lawyers use AI (say, to draft a brief or suggest a case strategy), the lawyer must review and approve the AI's output for accuracy and not rely on it blindly. The legal profession is building in such safeguards to uphold ethics – and the same concept applies to your business. Human oversight and good judgment are your best tools to mitigate AI's quirks.

Another crucial principle is transparency. Be open about how you're using AI, both internally and externally. Internally, make sure your team understands the AI tools you use and the dos and don'ts (e.g. "we use an AI scheduling assistant, but remember to check its invites for errors or odd times"). Externally, consider informing your customers in plain language when an AI is involved in serving them. If you have a chatbot on your website, you might say, "Hi, I'm AutoHelper, a virtual assistant. I can answer FAQs or take your message for the team." This kind of honesty helps manage expectations and builds trust. Customers generally don't mind AI assistance – what they dislike is feeling deceived. And if an AI makes a mistake in a customer interaction, being transparent makes it easier to apologize and fix it ("Sorry about that error – our automated system slipped up. We're reviewing it and a human staff member will help you now."). Ultimately, aligning your AI usage with your company's core values – fairness, transparency, quality, whatever they may be – is not just ethically right but *smart business*. When you use AI in a way that respects people and treats them fairly, you avoid ethical pitfalls and build trust with your customers. They'll see that you're using modern tools to serve them better, but not at the expense of their rights or dignity. A small business that gets this right can truly have the best of both worlds: cutting-edge efficiency with a conscience and personal touch.

Protecting Customer Data and Privacy

Small businesses often collect a *treasure trove* of personal data – email addresses, purchase histories, maybe even sensitive info like birthdays, health preferences, or financial details. When you bring AI into the mix, you'll likely be feeding this data into AI tools to get insights or automate tasks. That's powerful, but it also means you have to handle the data with extra care. In this section, we cover how to be a good steward of your customers' data and stay on the right side of privacy laws. The guiding principle here is to treat customer data as preciously as you'd want your own data treated. Misusing or carelessly handling personal data isn't just a potential legal violation – it's a fast way to lose customer trust.

First, let's talk about some common-sense privacy best practices. One is anonymizing or encrypting data before using it in AI tools whenever possible. If you're analyzing customer purchase patterns, does the AI really need to know each customer's name or email? Often it doesn't – it might only need IDs or aggregated info. By anonymizing data (removing personal identifiers) you reduce the risk *in case* there's ever a leak or misuse. Encryption is another layer – many AI tools or databases let you encrypt data, so even if someone unauthorized got it, they couldn't read it without the key. Another best practice: know your tools. Always read the terms of service and privacy policy of any third-party AI service you use. It might be tedious, but it's important to understand how they handle your data. Will they use the data you input to "train" their models or for other purposes? Reputable AI vendors often promise not to use your data to improve their models (especially if you pay for a business tier service). For example, OpenAI (the company behind ChatGPT) has a policy that by default it does not use business customers' data for training its AI models. Similarly, Microsoft's Azure OpenAI and other enterprise AI offerings boast that they have enterprise-grade security and will not retain or leak your inputs. But these assurances only apply if you're using the right service tiers and settings – hence the need to double-check. Choose AI vendors with strong security measures and good reputations. If an AI tool is free but from an unknown developer, think twice before feeding it your customer list. Sometimes it's worth paying a bit for a trusted platform that clearly states your data stays private.

Let's illustrate why this diligence matters. In 2023, Samsung had a mini-crisis when some of its engineers used ChatGPT to help with code, inadvertently pasting sensitive internal code into the chatbot. By doing so, they essentially handed confidential information to an external system. Samsung's reaction? They *banned* employees from using such AI tools on sensitive work devices after discovering a data leak resulted from code being input into ChatGPT. The incident highlighted that even well-meaning staff can accidentally compromise data if they're not careful about where they input it. For a small business, the lesson is: set clear guidelines for your team. If you allow using tools like ChatGPT or other AI on real customer data, make sure everyone knows what can and cannot be shared. You might decide, for example, that it's okay to use ChatGPT to brainstorm marketing copy, but not to paste in a private customer email to "draft a reply," unless you've confirmed the platform won't store or misuse that email.

Beyond best practices, you also need to be aware of privacy regulations that may apply to your business. Data protection laws are no longer just a big-business problem; they often apply based on *where your customers are*. Two of the biggest ones are GDPR and CCPA. GDPR (General Data Protection Regulation) is the European Union's strict data privacy law, and it can apply to you even if your business is not in Europe. If you have customers in the EU or are handling personal data of EU residents, GDPR's rules kick in. GDPR requires things like getting clear consent for collecting personal data, giving people the right to access or delete their data, and notifying authorities (and users) if sensitive data is breached. The penalties can be huge – up to €20 million or 4% of your global revenue, whichever is higher. Now, a small business might not face a multi-million euro fine (since fines are often proportional), but even fines in the thousands can hurt. And yes, small companies *have* been fined under GDPR. For example, a small UK marketing firm was fined around €200,000 for sending unsolicited marketing messages without proper consent. Others have been fined for things like failing to secure data or honor deletion requests. The point is, GDPR enforcement isn't only aimed at Fortune 500s – regulators will enforce rules on any size company if there's a complaint or violation.

CCPA (California Consumer Privacy Act) is a similar law but focused on California residents. CCPA mainly targets larger businesses (those with revenues above $25M, or dealing in large amounts of personal data), but even if you're below those thresholds, it's influencing privacy standards across the U.S. CCPA gives California consumers rights to know what data you collect about them, to opt out of having their data sold, and to request deletion of their data (with some exceptions). Importantly, if you *do* fall under CCPA's scope and don't comply, fines can be steep – up to $2,500 per violation (or up to $7,500 per intentional violation), *per consumer, per incident.* "Per incident" can add up fast – e.g., if you improperly leaked 100 customers' data, that might be 100 incidents.

In one notable case, the popular videoconferencing company Zoom agreed to an $85 million settlement for CCPA-related issues around user data handling. While Zoom is huge, the lesson trickles down: regulators and consumers expect businesses of all sizes to handle personal data carefully.

So what do you, as a small business owner, actually need to do to protect privacy and comply with these laws? Here's a quick plain-language checklist:

- Obtain proper consent: Don't collect personal data without permission. If you have a newsletter sign-up, use clear language like "Enter your email to receive updates" – and avoid pre-ticked checkboxes (GDPR hates those). For any sensitive data, be extra explicit about why you need it.

- Allow opt-outs and deletions: Make it easy for customers to say "no thanks" to data collection or marketing. Provide an unsubscribe link in emails. Under laws like GDPR/CCPA, if a customer asks "Delete all my info you have," you likely need to do it (barring legitimate needs like an ongoing contract or legal obligation to keep records). Having a process for this – even if it's just an email contact for privacy requests – is important.

- Minimize data collection: Don't hoard data you don't need. If you run a small e-commerce shop that ships physical goods, you obviously need addresses to deliver – but you probably *don't* need to collect, say, the customer's birthdate or annual income unless it's integral to your service. The idea of "data minimization" is both a legal and ethical guideline: collect only what you need, and don't keep it longer than necessary.

- Secure your data: Use up-to-date security measures to store customer information. This means things like strong passwords, encryption, keeping your software patched, etc. A huge chunk (over 80% in 2024) of GDPR fines were due to companies not preventing data breaches or leaks. Even a small leak (like leaving a database unprotected online) can lead to penalties and definitely a loss of trust. If you're using cloud tools, ensure they are reputable and have security certifications.

- Know your vendors: If you upload customer data to an AI tool or any third-party service, that service is effectively your "data processor" under laws like GDPR. You should use vendors that either certify their compliance or at least clearly state how they protect data. Many AI service providers offer data processing addendums or agreements for GDPR – don't be afraid to reach out to them or check their compliance pages.

The upside of all this? By treating customer data with utmost sensitivity and following privacy best practices, you *not only avoid legal trouble* – you gain customer confidence. In an era of daily news about data breaches and abuses, customers really value businesses that show they respect privacy. It can become a selling point: you might mention in your marketing, "We respect your privacy – we will never sell your data, and we only use your information to serve you better." When leveraging AI, emphasize that it's *in service of the customer*: for instance, "We use AI to recommend products you'll love, but rest assured, your data is kept secure and private." This kind of messaging, backed up by genuine action, can turn AI from a potential concern into a trust-building advantage.

Navigating the Regulatory Landscape for AI

It seems like every week there's a news headline about governments waking up to AI – sometimes praising its potential, other times warning of its risks. As a small business owner implementing AI, you don't need to become a policy wonk, but you do need a basic awareness of the rules and guidelines that are emerging. Think of it this way: just as you keep an eye on tax rules or industry-specific regulations that affect your business, keeping an eye on AI-related rules is now part of the game. This section provides an overview of the current and upcoming regulations that might affect your AI strategy, and some practical steps to stay compliant without losing your sanity.

One of the most significant efforts is happening across the Atlantic with the European Union's proposed AI Act. Why care about a European law if you're not in Europe? Two reasons: First, if you use AI in a way that affects people in the EU (say you have some EU customers, or you use an AI tool provided by an EU company), you may need to comply. Second, the EU AI Act is seen as a trailblazer – it's likely to influence other jurisdictions and become a model for future laws elsewhere. The EU AI Act takes a *risk-based approach*. It will categorize AI uses by risk level: *unacceptable risk* (uses that are banned outright), *high-risk* (uses that are allowed but heavily regulated), and lower risk (with fewer requirements). For example, AI systems that fall under "unacceptable" might include things like social scoring (à la Black Mirror episodes) or real-time facial recognition in public places – these are likely to be prohibited in the EU. "High-risk" categories include areas like recruitment, credit scoring, healthcare diagnostics, and other sensitive uses where an AI's decision can seriously impact someone's life. If a small business in the EU (or serving EU folks) uses an AI for hiring or lending decisions, that AI tool might be considered high-risk. What does that mean? Under the AI Act, high-risk AI systems will have to meet certain requirements – think of things like documentation of how they work, transparency to users, and even possibly having human oversight mechanisms. The obligations largely fall on the providers of the AI system (the companies that create the software), but as the user of a high-risk AI, you would also have duties – such as monitoring the outcomes and using the system as intended. While at the time of writing the EU AI Act is not law yet, it's on the horizon. The message it sends is: regulators don't want to ban AI for businesses, but they do want to ensure AI is used safely, fairly, and transparently, especially in critical areas.

Meanwhile, in the United States, there isn't a single all-encompassing federal AI law (yet). But that doesn't mean it's a wild west. U.S. regulators are applying *existing laws* to AI scenarios, and some states and cities are enacting their own rules. For instance, remember the earlier discussion about biased hiring AI? In 2023, the U.S. Equal Employment Opportunity Commission (EEOC) brought its first AI-related discrimination case, against a company whose recruiting software was automatically rejecting older applicants. The company, an online tutoring firm, ended up settling and paying out to the rejected candidates. The takeaway: even without a new "AI law," the same old laws against discrimination or unfair practices apply to AI. If your AI tool ends up discriminating, you could be held responsible under laws like the Civil Rights Act, Americans with Disabilities Act, or other anti-bias regulations, just as if a human manager made those biased decisions. The EEOC, the Federal Trade Commission (FTC), the Department of Justice – these agencies have all issued statements that basically say, "Hey, just because you use an algorithm doesn't mean you're off the hook. We will hold you accountable for what your AI does". The FTC in particular has been vocal: they've warned businesses that using AI that is deceptive or discriminatory in how it targets consumers could be seen as an unfair business practice. In plain terms, if your AI does something that would be illegal for a person to do, it's still illegal when an AI does it.

On top of that, we see *sector-specific guidelines* emerging. In New York City, a new law came into effect that requires companies to audit their AI hiring tools for bias and *notify* job candidates if AI was used in evaluating them. In the legal industry, as we noted, bar associations in states like California and New York are telling lawyers they must supervise AI outputs and even inform clients if AI was used in a legal task. The medical field too is grappling with AI: for example, the FDA (Food & Drug Administration) has to approve certain AI-driven medical devices or diagnostic tools, and medical associations emphasize that doctors should validate AI-driven diagnoses. If you're in finance and using AI for, say, loan decisions or stock advice, expect guidelines from financial regulators about transparency and fairness (the U.S. Consumer Financial Protection Bureau has already said lenders can't use black-box algorithms to hide discriminatory practices). The bottom line is, regulation isn't meant to scare you away from AI, but to make sure it's used responsibly. It's similar to how food businesses have health codes – they're not there to stop people from cooking, just to ensure the kitchen is clean!

So how can a small business owner stay on top of compliance without feeling overwhelmed? A few practical tips:

- Do your due diligence on AI tools. Before using an AI application, especially for something high-stakes like hiring or analyzing personal data, check if the vendor provides any compliance info. Do they mention bias testing or compliance with laws? If an AI tool is meant for HR, does it say it's EEOC compliant or has been audited for bias? Using reputable tools can put you on safer ground.

- Keep records and logs of how you use AI for important decisions. If an AI makes a recommendation on something major (like rejecting a loan application), log that recommendation and the factors behind it, in case you ever need to explain it. Some AI systems will provide explanation data – if available, save it. This kind of record-keeping is useful if you're ever questioned on why a decision was made. It's also just good practice to periodically review those logs yourself to spot any weird patterns.

- Stay updated, but don't panic. You don't need to read every AI law blog, but do keep an ear out in your industry community. If you're a small healthcare provider, for instance, pay attention if your professional association issues AI usage guidelines. If you're using AI in marketing, follow the FTC's business updates (they occasionally post blog guidance for businesses regarding AI). Consider signing up for a newsletter or two that digest AI regulation news for laypeople. The landscape is evolving, but major changes usually come with grace periods and lots of press. If you stay generally informed, you'll have time to adapt.

- When in doubt, err on the side of transparency and caution. If you're unsure whether you need to inform people about AI usage, it's often better to do it. If you're not sure if an AI's output might be infringing on something (like maybe it scraped content from somewhere), maybe don't use that output blindly. A little caution can save a lot of headaches.

The encouraging thing is that regulators have also acknowledged they want to help small businesses innovate with AI, not stifle them. For example, the EU AI Act discussions include provisions to support small and medium enterprises in compliance, such as offering sandboxes (testing environments) and possibly reduced requirements for smaller scope activities. And if you do business in multiple regions, you might find that complying with the strictest law that applies to you (say GDPR) will by extension put you in good shape for others. Much like how many websites just apply GDPR standards globally now (instead of having one standard for Europe and a lax one elsewhere), you might choose to adopt a high bar for AI ethics and privacy across your operations – and then you don't have to worry as much about the patchwork of rules.

In short, a proactive approach to compliance turns it from a scary unknown into a manageable part of your AI strategy. By keeping an eye on the rules, using AI tools wisely, and documenting what you do, even a tiny company can confidently deploy AI without running afoul of the law. Remember, laws and regulations ultimately aim to ensure AI is used safely and transparently – which is aligned with running a trustworthy business anyway. Use that as your compass, and you'll likely be ahead of the curve.

Building Trust through Transparency and Accountability

At the end of the day, small businesses thrive on trust – the personal relationships, community reputation, and word-of-mouth goodwill that giant corporations often struggle to maintain. So how does AI fit into that picture? When implemented thoughtfully, AI can actually *enhance* your small business's trust factor – by improving service and consistency – but only if you remain transparent and accountable in its use. This final section ties together everything we've discussed about ethics and compliance into one overarching goal: maintaining and even building trust with your customers, employees, and partners as you integrate AI into your business.

One key strategy is openness about AI usage. Rather than using AI in the shadows and hoping nobody notices, be upfront and frame it as a positive. For example, let's say you add an AI chatbot to your website to answer common customer questions. Introduce it to your customers: "Meet Anna, our 24/7 virtual assistant. She can instantly help answer your FAQs or take your message if it's after hours." By clearly informing customers when they are interacting with an AI (and giving it a friendly persona), you demystify the experience. Customers are far less likely to feel deceived or frustrated, and more likely to appreciate the instant help. Importantly, also provide an option to reach a human if needed. Many companies do this with a simple button or prompt: "Would you like to speak with a human? Click here." Even if 90% of people stick with the AI for quick answers, knowing that a human is behind the curtain if things get complicated provides reassurance. It says, "We're using smart tools to help you faster, but we're *not* ignoring the human touch."

Speaking of the human touch, it's vital to emphasize within your team and to your customers that AI is a tool to assist your team, not replace it. In a small business, every employee often wears multiple hats and builds personal rapport with customers. You don't want AI to erode that. Instead, integrate AI in ways that free your people to do more of what humans do best. For instance, if AI handles appointment scheduling or basic customer questions, your staff has more time to give undivided attention to clients who have complex needs or to add creative flair to projects. You can even highlight this: "Thanks to our new AI scheduler, Jane (our office manager) has more time to personally ensure every event we plan for you is unique and special." This way, customers see AI as an enhancement to your service, not a cold replacement. It also sets the right expectation that if something is emotionally nuanced or requires judgment, a human is in charge. In fact, experts often note that AI cannot replace uniquely human qualities like judgment, empathy, creativity, and relationship-building. A recent MIT Sloan study underscored that tasks relying on empathy and ethical judgment are *least* likely to be automated by AI. AI excels at routine tasks and data analysis – crunching numbers, sorting information, answering straightforward queries – which can significantly augment what humans can do. But only humans can truly understand another person's feelings, think outside the box in ambiguous situations, or build a trusted relationship over time.

Let's consider a small fictional example. Imagine "Bright Blooms," a local flower shop that decides to use AI in a few ways. They have an AI tool that manages their inventory (so customers are less likely to find a certain bouquet out of stock) and an AI chatbot on their website that helps people place orders after hours. Bright Blooms openly tells customers about these additions: a little note on their website says, "We've implemented a smart assistant to help serve you 24/7 and ensure we always have the freshest flowers in stock using predictive ordering." Customers start noticing that when they call the shop, the florist isn't scrambling checking stock – she already knows what's available (thanks to AI alerts). And if they message the chatbot at 11pm to order Mother's Day flowers, it works smoothly, and the next morning a friendly human follows up with a personal confirmation. The shop also posts on social media a behind-the-scenes story: "Fun fact: we use an AI to help us predict how many roses to stock for Valentine's Day, but *don't worry*, it's still Hannah and Mary who do the beautiful arrangements by hand!" This kind of transparency turns AI into part of the brand story – one that says "we're innovative and efficient *and* we maintain our personal touch." It builds trust because customers don't feel anything is hidden, and they see the *accountability*: humans are still overseeing everything.

Accountability is the other side of the coin. Being accountable means if the AI makes a mistake, you take responsibility and fix it. Small businesses can actually shine here because you're close to your customers. If your AI recommendation engine suggests an utterly wrong product to a customer, you can reach out and say, "Oops, our new system missed the mark there – we're sorry for the confusion, and we've taken your feedback to heart to improve it. Meanwhile, Janet from our team has picked out an item she thinks you'll love." By acknowledging the issue and making it right, you not only salvage the situation, you potentially deepen the customer's trust (they see that you care and respond quickly). In contrast, big corporations sometimes hide behind faceless systems and can frustrate customers with a lack of recourse. Your small business advantage is that you can combine AI efficiency with genuine accountability and customer care. If you hold yourself to high standards – auditing your AI processes regularly, being willing to tweak or shut off an AI feature that isn't working right – people will notice. It shows you're using AI *intentionally*, not just as a gimmick or cost-cutting shortcut.

Finally, it's worth reiterating a reassuring fact: AI will never have a warm smile, a firm handshake, or the ability to truly understand someone's unique life story. Those are your domain. As much as AI advances, it's there to handle the heavy lifting and the grunt work. It can analyze a thousand survey responses in a flash and tell you "customers mostly mention 'price' and 'selection' as issues." But it will be a human on your team who reads that and says, "Alright, how do we empathize and creatively solve this?" Experts in AI and business consistently emphasize that the winning formula is "AI + human," not AI alone.

When customers experience a service that seamlessly blends efficiency with empathy, they feel they're getting the best of both worlds. Imagine a future where your small company can deliver *big-company* precision and speed (because your AI systems are humming in the background ensuring nothing falls through the cracks), *while still delivering small-company friendliness and personal attention.* That's not a distant dream – that's the Small Business AI Advantage you've been reading about throughout this book.

In conclusion, safeguarding your AI strategy with ethics, privacy, compliance, and transparency isn't just about avoiding pitfalls – it's about actively building a business that people trust and love. By integrating AI in a way that highlights human oversight and empathy, you demonstrate that you're not using technology for its own sake, but to *better serve* your customers and community. A small business that is AI-enabled and run ethically and transparently truly has a competitive edge. You can deliver the efficiency and capabilities that once only big companies had, while preserving the authenticity, accountability, and care that define beloved small businesses. Do this, and you're not just competing with the Fortune 500s – you're outclassing them on both tech and heart. Here's to your journey in leveraging AI responsibly, and to the trust and success that will follow!

Epilogue

The small business landscape has fundamentally shifted. What once required massive capital investments, entire IT departments, and Fortune 500 budgets now sits within reach of every entrepreneur with vision and determination. Artificial intelligence has become the great equalizer, transforming how businesses operate, compete, and thrive.

Throughout these pages, we've explored the practical pathways to AI implementation—from automating customer service with chatbots to optimizing inventory management through predictive analytics. These tools represent more than technological advancement; they embody opportunity itself. The corner bakery can now predict demand patterns with the same sophistication as multinational chains. The freelance consultant can deliver enterprise-level insights using free AI platforms. The family-run manufacturer can streamline operations with intelligence that rivals industry giants.

The democratization of AI has arrived, and small businesses stand to benefit most. While corporations navigate bureaucracy and legacy systems, nimble entrepreneurs can implement AI solutions overnight. This agility becomes your competitive advantage—the ability to adapt, experiment, and innovate without the constraints that burden larger organizations.

Success with AI requires commitment to continuous learning and strategic thinking. The landscape evolves rapidly, but the fundamentals remain: start small, measure results, and scale gradually. Each automated process creates capacity for higher-value work. Every optimization generates resources for further growth.

The future belongs to businesses that embrace intelligent automation while maintaining human creativity and connection. AI amplifies your capabilities without replacing your unique value proposition. Your expertise, combined with artificial intelligence, creates possibilities that neither could achieve alone.

The tools are ready. The opportunity is unprecedented. Your journey toward AI-powered growth begins now, and the potential for transformation has never been greater.

www.ingramcontent.com/pod-product-compliance
Lightning Source LLC
Chambersburg PA
CBHW071427210326
41597CB00020B/3687